TRACKING THE
MAN-BEASTS

TRACKING THE
MAN-BEASTS

SASQUATCH,
VAMPIRES,
ZOMBIES,
AND MORE

JOE NICKELL

Prometheus Books

59 John Glenn Drive
Amherst, New York 14228–2119

Published 2011 by Prometheus Books

Cover image features an endangered Northern Hairy-Nosed Wombat footprint
in sand (Epping National Park, Scientific, Queensland, Australia).

Cover image © 2011 Media Bakery, Inc.
Cover design by Grace M. Conti-Zilsberger.

Inquiries should be addressed to
Prometheus Books
59 John Glenn Drive
Amherst, New York 14228–2119
VOICE: 716–691–0133
FAX: 716–691–0137
WWW.PROMETHEUSBOOKS.COM

15 14 13 12 11   5 4 3 2 1

Library of Congress Cataloging-in-Publication Data

Nickell, Joe.
    Tracking the man-beasts : Sasquatch, vampires, zombies, and more / by Joe
Nickell.
        p. cm.
    Includes index.
    ISBN 978–1–61614–415–9 (pbk. : alk. paper)
    ISBN 978–1–61614–416–6 (e-book)
    1. Monsters. 2. Animals, Mythical. 3. Extraterrestrial beings. I. Title.

QL89.N65 2011
001.944—dc22

                                                                    2010047320

Printed in the United States of America on acid-free paper

Contents

Acknowledgments

A book such as this could not be done without the help of many individuals.

I am especially grateful to Paul Kurtz, chairman and founder of Prometheus Books, for believing in this project; John and Mary Frantz for financial support for my investigations; the editors and artists at Prometheus, who shepherded this project through the editorial process, especially Steven L. Mitchell, Ian Birnbaum, Jade Zora Ballard, Brian McMahon, Cate Roberts-Abel, and Grace M. Conti-Zilsberger; Timothy Binga, director of the Center for Inquiry Libraries, for research assistance; Paul E. Loynes for typesetting; and indeed the entire Center for Inquiry (CFI) and *Skeptical Inquirer* staff for help at all levels—especially Ronald A. Lindsay, president and CEO of CFI; Barry Karr, executive director of CFI's Committee for Skeptical Inquiry; and Kendrick Frazier, editor of the *Skeptical Inquirer* (CFI's science magazine). My wife, Diana Gawen Harris, also helped in ways too numerous to mention.

In addition to those mentioned in the text, I am further indebted to many folklorists, historians, popular writers, librarians, television producers, town clerks, and other generous folk who assisted me in my work over the many years of this investigative pursuit.

Introduction

If much evidence is to be believed, the creatures of our natural world coexist with many extranatural ones, not only ghosts and angels but also monstrous beings that lurk at the very fringes of science. Are they real—denizens of unexplored regions or even supernatural realms? Or are they only creatures of our prolific imagination?

The Lure of Monsters

Just what *are* monsters? Definitions vary, but most sources agree that they are creatures of great size or deformity, or are part human and part animal, or have some aspect of horror or wonder. (See for example *Webster's New Twentieth-Century Dictionary* 1980.) At least one source suggests a monster is "an imaginary creature" (*DK Illustrated Oxford Dictionary* 1998).

Whether ultimately real or not, monsters concern us. They are mysterious beings that range from the beneficent to the fearsome to the merely strange. That is, they are in some way expressions of our greatest hopes and deepest fears, as well as our insatiable curiosity. If they aren't really real, we seem to think, they ought to be!

Some monsters are seen in an especially hopeful light. Extraterrestrial beings, for example, like angels, imply that we are not alone in the universe. Other monsters offer different affirmations: for instance, the survival of a creature presumably like a plesiosaur (an extinct marine animal) in Lake Champlain—affectionately nicknamed "Champ" (Radford and Nickell 2006, 27)—would be especially welcome in our shrinking world where so many life-forms have become extinct.

On the flip side are horrific entities that lurk in the shadows of our subconscious, feeding on our most primal fears. Daniel Cohen, author of *Supermonsters* (1977, 5), concedes, "I don't know why we enjoy things that scare us, but we do." I have a notion why, which I developed out of my years on carnival midways (Nickell 2005). There, juxtaposed with thrill rides (from the classic Tilt-A-Whirl to the looping roller coaster), were various scare shows. These included "Haunted Mansion" (a spook show in a trailer) and even sideshow attractions like "Atasha the Gorilla Girl." (This featured a beauty-to-beast "transformation"—actually an illusion effected with a mirror—that sent spectators fleeing for the exit [Nickell 2005, 288].) Both the thrill rides and the scare shows elicited squeals and screams from patrons—evidence, I take it, that chills *are* thrills, both of which provide an enjoyable adrenaline "rush."

Hence, scary monsters are good for around-the-campfire stories, but they are by no means limited to such vicarious pleasures. Adults sometimes utilize them as bogeymen to frighten children into behaving or perhaps into keeping close to home. As well, religious authorities have unleashed demons and devils on their adult congregations for similar purposes.

Some monstrous beings spark both our hopes and our fears as well as provoke our curiosity. For example, we wonder if extraterrestrials actually exist and, if so, whether they have visited us. We suppose that they could be our potential friends and allies (the message of Steven Spielberg's 1982 movie, *E.T.: The Extra-Terrestrial*) or that they might instead be predatory, as witness the modern profusion of "alien abduction" claims (Nickell 2007, 251–58). We seem especially attracted to—or repelled by—beings that in some way resemble us.

In Our Image

According to the first chapter of the Old Testament book of Genesis, "God created man in his *own* image, in the image of God created he him" (1:27). But was not it really the other way around? Religions have traditionally adopted anthropomorphism, that is, have attributed human form or qualities to deities and other mythological entities. Thus in Genesis, God "breathed" into man's nostrils the "breath of life" (3:8); went "walking" in the garden of Eden (3:8), where his "voice" was heard speaking the language of humans; grieved "at his heart" over man's wickedness (5:6); and so on. (This is the anthropomorphic God depicted in Michelangelo's *Creation of Man* mural on the ceiling of the Sistine Chapel.) Other supernatural beings in the Old Testament—including Satan and angels—are similarly given human attributes.

In ancient mythology, anthropomorphism is often seen in the form of hybrids: composite figures that are part human, part animal. The Egyptians, Greeks, and others envisioned such hybrids in their pantheons of gods—sphinxes and satyrs among them.

As an extension of the impulse to imagine humanlike monsters, just as human qualities and forms were attributed to supernatural beings, so were abnormal humans termed *monstrosities*. They were often held to presage disaster or were seen as evidence of divine wrath. Some believed that they were the result of mating with animals. Often, such beings—those like modern sideshow "freaks" called "alligator" boys and girls (who suffer from extreme ichthyosis) or "frog" people (e.g., a hunchback midget)—might be put to death (Thompson 1968, 17).

Then there are those archetypal human-turned-monster entities who have frightened generation after generation. From Mary Shelley's *Frankenstein* (1818) and Bram Stoker's *Dracula* (1897) to Robert Louis Stevenson's psychological classic, *The Strange Case of Dr. Jekyll and Mr. Hyde* (1886), literary monsters have helped spawn numerous movie creatures like *The Wolfman* (1941). These, in turn, are rivaled by such real-life, if figurative, man-beasts, including Jack the Ripper, who slashed and disemboweled prostitutes in London in 1888, and the ghoulish Jeffrey Dahmer, who not only engaged in cannibalism but also attempted to create "zombies" as sex playthings by drilling holes in the victims' skull and dribbling in caustic chemicals (Newton 2000, 46–48, 112–15).

Today, there is a special fascination with humanlike creatures that seem to bracket us in time. Extraterrestrials tend to be *humanoids* that represent advanced civilizations, while various other humanlike creatures appear to be evolutionary throwbacks. These include the ubiquitous "Wild Man of the Woods" and various apelike creatures, including the Abominable Snowman.

In short, monsters are frequently modeled on ourselves. Just as we imagine that angels are us with wings, Bigfoot is our stupid cousin from the past, extraterrestrials are our futuristic selves, and werewolves and vampires are us with an attitude!

Investigation

While monsters are often consigned to ancient legend and literary fiction—in other words, supposed realms of the imagination—many are held to be in some sense real. Such paranormal beings (those beyond the normal range of science and human experience) include supernatural ones, such as the werewolf, as well as others (like the Yowie, Australia's version of Bigfoot) that, if they indeed exist, could be perfectly natural creatures; these are embraced by cryptozoology, the study of unknown or "hidden" creatures (i.e., cryptids).

I have been studying these and other reputed paranormalities for some four decades, beginning in 1969, when I sat in my first séance to attempt to contact the spirit of Houdini. By 1995 I had become, apparently, the world's only full-time professional paranormal investigator, turning my reports into articles for *Skeptical Inquirer* science magazine and then into chapters of books (e.g., Nickell 2001, 2007).

Along the way, I have studied mythological, folkloric, and literary monsters (in both undergraduate and graduate courses); traveled to many remote regions in search of legendary creatures, including Argentina's Chupacabra, Australia's Yowie, and Austria's werewolf (not even to exhaust the *A*'s); sought vampire graves in Vermont; visited numerous carnival midways to meet human "monsters," look behind the scenes at exhibited spider-women and the like, and witness the transformation of a lovely girl into a wild gorilla; examined one museum's "mermaid," another's "alien hybrid," and still another's allegedly petrified "Cardiff Giant"; became "animal trainer for a day" at an aquarium, where I interacted with creatures that can be mistaken for monsters; went on a nighttime expedition with Bigfoot hunters; explored the Pacific Bigfoot country; conducted photographic and other experiments; and collected monster track-casts and curios for my online Skeptiseum (http://www.skeptiseum.org/).

In addition, I have listened patiently to various monster eyewitnesses, including "alien abductees"; conversed with psychologists and wildlife biologists; pried secrets from sideshow "gaff" artists (creators of fake exhibits); and debated fellow cryptozoologists and monsterologists. I have visited legendary monster sites, accompanying film crews for television-documentary series like the History Channel's *Monster Quest* and National Geographic's *Is It Real?* and I have spent countless hours in libraries and other research facilities to glean monster-related facts (concerning Mothman's eyeshine, for instance). I have engaged in many other monster pursuits, sharing my findings with newspaper, radio, television, and Internet audiences, and I have lectured at venues ranging from schools and summer camps to scholarly meetings and scientific conferences.

In my investigations, I have relied on some fundamental principles. One is that "extraordinary claims require extraordinary proof"—an old skeptical maxim. In other words, evidence must be commensurate with a given claim.

Another principle is that the burden of proof is on the advocate of a claim, not on anyone who would question it (since it is difficult or even impossible to prove a negative). This is an established principle in law, science, and scholarship.

Still another principle, called Occam's razor (named for fourteenth-century philosopher William of Ockham), holds that the simplest tenable explanation—that is, the one with the fewest assumptions—is most likely to be correct. It is not, of course, a guarantee of absolute truth but rather a prescription for determining the preferred hypothesis among competing hypotheses.

In the pages that follow, we set out to track the man-beasts—to separate fact from fancy. We will be on an open-minded quest to investigate mysterious sightings, physical traces, and other evidence, following along the trail of mystery. Let us emulate Sherlock Holmes, who said in *The Hound of the Baskervilles*, "We balance probabilities and choose the most likely. It is the scientific use of the imagination."

References

Cohen, Daniel. 1977. *Supermonsters*. New York: Pocket Books.

DK Publishing. 1998. *DK Illustrated Oxford Dictionary*. New York: DK Publishing.

Newton, Michael. 2000. *The Encyclopedia of Serial Killers*. New York: Checkmark Books.

Nickell, Joe. 1993. *Looking for a Miracle: Weeping Icons, Relics, Stigmata, Visions and Healing Cures*. Amherst, NY: Prometheus Books.

———. 1995. *Entities: Angels, Spirits, Demons, and Other Alien Beings*. Amherst, NY: Prometheus Books.

———. 2001. "Phantoms, Frauds, or Fantasies?" *Hauntings and Poltergeists: Multidisciplinary Perspectives*, edited by James Houran and Rense Lange, 214–24. Jefferson, NC: McFarland.

———. 2007. *Adventures in Paranormal Investigation*. Lexington, KY: University Press of Kentucky.

Radford, Benjamin, and Joe Nickell. 2006. *Lake Monster Mysteries: Investigating the World's Most Elusive Creatures*. Lexington, KY: University Press of Kentucky.

Summers, Montague. 1996. *The Werewolf*. New York: Bell Publishing.
Thompson, C. J. S. 1968. *Giants, Dwarfs, and Other Oddities*. New York: University Books.
Webster's New Twentieth Century Dictionary, Unabridged. 2nd ed. 1980. Cleveland, OH: William Collins.

Part I
"Monster" Men

Chapter 1

Monstrosities

From ancient history, abnormal creatures—both animal and human—were termed *monstrosities*. The births of these so-called monsters were typically explained in superstitious terms that invoked the supernatural: they were held to presage disaster or thought to be evidence of divine judgment. Some thought they resulted from mating with animals (Thompson 1968, 17). Often, they were put to death (Fiedler 1993, 21) (see figure 1.1).

Between discussions of "an infant born with two heads" and "a monster with four arms and four feet endowed with but one head" (from today's perspective, obviously the result of incomplete separation of a single, fertilized egg), seventeenth-century writer John Bulwer (1653) commented, "these apparitions that be contrarie to nature, happen not without the providence of Almighty God, but for the punishing and admonishing of men, these things by just judgment are often permitted, not but that man hath a great hand in these monstrosities." He did note that the "monster" with eight limbs, "being baptized," had "lived some time afterwards."

Human Monsters

Among the earliest records of monstrosities, ancient Babylonian texts show that those in the form of newborn infants were among the divinatory

Figure 1.1: Human "monsters" are depicted in this woodcut of 1499.

images consulted by astrologers. Here is a selection from some of the texts (translated from cuneiform writing impressed into clay tablets) from circa 2800 BCE:

> When a woman gives birth to an infant;—that has the ears of a lion; there will be a powerful King in the country. . . .
> That has a bird's beak; the country will be peaceful. . . .
> That has no well-marked sex; calamity and affliction will seize upon the land. . . .
> That has no feet; the canals of the country will be cut (intercepted) and the house ruined. . . .

Other references in the Babylonian texts are to "six toes on each foot," "the right foot in the form of a fish's tail," and many others, including "three feet, two in their normal position (attached to the body) and the third between them" (quoted in Thompson 1968, 25–29). The last mentioned, for example, is reminiscent of the modern oddity Francesco A. "Frank" Lentini (1889–1966), billed in circus sideshows as the "Three-Legged Wonder" (Nickell 2005, 131–32). Such similarities between past and present oddities confirm that many of the same deformities were known nearly five millennia ago.

Still later, as Thompson (1968, 30) observes:

> The curious beliefs that gathered round the occurrence of monsters in early times were common also among the ancient Greeks and Romans, and there is ample evidence of this in the mythological stories in such impossible beings as centaurs, fauns with extremities like goats, and creatures with pectoral eyes, syrens, nereids, double-headed monsters and the other fearsome creatures that play a prominent part in many of their legends and traditions.

("Syrens" [or sirens] and nereids were sea nymphs.)

Exhibited "Freaks"

Over the centuries, there are few certain records of monstrosities until the close of the eleventh century. However, in the year 945, a pair of Armenian boys joined at their abdomens (very much like the later "Siamese twins," Chang and Eng Bunker, once exhibited by P. T. Barnum) were exhibited in Constantinople. "They excited great interest and curiosity," remarks

Thompson (1968, 30–31), "but they were removed by order of the authorities, as it was considered at the time that such abnormal creatures presaged evil."

In later circuses and carnivals, such human oddities were termed *freaks* (as in freaks of nature) and were exhibited in what were typically called *freak shows*. Fiedler (1993, 23–24) observed that, beyond the merely disabled, "[o]nly the true freak challenges the conventional boundaries between male and female, sexed and sexless, animal and human, large and small, self and other, and consequently between reality and illusion, experience and fantasy, fact and myth."

Whatever their era, examples of human monstrosities include midgets and dwarfs at one end of the size spectrum and giants at the other. (These will be discussed in chapters 2 and 3, respectively.) Other examples are conjoined twins (like those already described), hirsute people (especially those entirely covered with long hair), and certain others regarded as human-animal hybrids (see part 5).

Of course, there have been exaggerated descriptions of monstrosities, many occurring over time due to processes well known to folklorists. Moreover, those fantastic creatures represented in monster books were often "repetitions, depicted with greater freedom of imagination, of those described in earlier times" (Thompson 1968, 30).

Real or Fake?

There have also been outright fakes, like the infant exhibited at Paris in 1593 with an enormous head. A suspicious magistrate investigated, and soon the parents confessed that they had made an incision in the crown for the insertion of a reed, and—having blown into it in increments over some months (using wax to seal up the hole)—had inflated the baby's head to grotesque proportions. The parents were executed for their crime (Hildanus n.d.).

Some persons even mutilated themselves in order to become fake beggars. One at Anjou in 1525 hid his own arm behind his back and exhibited a mutilated counterfeit cut from the body of a hanged man. He received much money until, one day, his counterfeit appendage accidentally fell on the ground and he was exposed. He was jailed, being later "whipped through the town with his false arm hanging before him and so banished" (Paré 1573). There were many others (Paré 1573):

Such as feign themselves dumb, draw back and double their tongues in their mouths. Such as fall down counterfeiting the falling sickness [epilepsy], bind straightly both their wrists with plates of iron, tumble or roll themselves in the mire, sprinkle and defile their faces with beasts' blood and shake their limbs and whole body.

Lastly, by putting soap into their mouths, they foam at the mouth like those that have falling sickness. Others, some with flour, make a kind of glue, wherewith they besmear their whole bodies as if they had leprosy.

The later sideshows were likewise a venue for imposters. "Gaffed" (faked) oddities included bogus Siamese twins, notably Adolph and Rudolph about the end of the nineteenth century. (A harness, concealed under a specially devised suit, held Rudolph so he appeared to grow from Adolph's waist.) There were also gaffed hermaphrodites, "gorilla" and "lion-faced" girls, and many more (Nickell 2005, 194–201).

As all these examples show, many of the man-beasts that continue to populate books on strange creatures have similar antecedents in the form of real human "monsters"—dating back to remote antiquity and continuing (while metamorphosing) into our supposedly more enlightened era.

References

Bulwer, John. 1653. *Changeling*. London: J. Hardesty. Cited in Thompson 1968, pp. 43, 246 (below).

Fiedler, Leslie. 1993. *Freaks: Myths and Images of the Secret Self*. New York: Anchor Books.

Hildanus, Frabricius. N.d. Cited in Thompson 1968, pp. 97–98 (below).

Nickell, Joe. 2005. *Secrets of the Sideshows*. Lexington, KY: University Press of Kentucky.

Paré, Abroise. 1573. Quoted in Thompson 1968, p. 96 (below).

Thompson, C. J. S. 1968. *The Mystery and Lore of Monsters*. New York: University Books.

Chapter 2

Dwarfs among Us

Among the numerous creatures of legend are the fairies. Deriving from the Latin word *fata* ("fate"), the term *fairy* denotes a group of supernatural beings who live near, and interact with, men and women (Guiley 1991, 198). These folkloric beings are assigned the ability to become invisible (as by donning a magical cap), and they perform acts of kindness (such as rescuing a lady imprisoned by her jealous husband) as well as punishment (perhaps knocking pans from kitchen shelves for failure to set out food and drink for them). In the past they were also said to have kidnapped mortals and to have taken them to the fairies' subterranean abode (in obvious parallels to today's reported alien abductions) (Leach 1984, 363–65).

In addition to various types of fairies, other little people include leprechauns (fairy associates in Ireland), elves (mischievous spritelike beings), pixies (diminutive field sprites), brownies (storybook elfin entities who do good deeds at night), and others—including, of course, dwarfs.

Fanciful and Real

In folklore, dwarfs are diminutive entities who are sometimes identified as trolls (impish cave dwellers) and sometimes as gnomes (misshapen dwarfs)— all supernatural beings who are said to inhabit the underground. Although they resemble men, their skin is wrinkled and leathery, and they have wide mouths and long beards. They may be seen by those with vivid imaginations—especially children or adults with fantasy-prone personalities, that is, otherwise normal people with an unusual ability to fantasize (Wilson and Barber 1983; Nickell 1995, 40–42, 268). The folklorist Reverend S. Baring-Gould described an encounter he had with dwarfs as a child (quoted in Doyle 1921, 129):

> In the year 1838, when I was a small boy of four years old, we were driving to Montpelier on a hot summer day over the long straight road that traverses a pebble-and-rubble-strewn plain, on which grows nothing save a few aromatic herbs. I was sitting on the box with my father when, to my great surprise, I saw legions of dwarfs of about two feet high running along beside the horses; some sat laughing on the pole, some were scrambling up the harness to get on the backs of the horses. I remarked to my father what I saw, when he abruptly stopped the carriage and put me inside beside my mother, where, the conveyance being closed, I was out of the sun. The effect was that, little by little, the host of imps diminished in number till they disappeared altogether.

But there are *real* dwarfs, of course, those people having the condition known as dwarfism, which may result from genetic defects or endocrine or nutritional deficiencies, or a combination of factors. Early writers did not differentiate between the various types of conspicuously small persons, but they include *Pygmies* (a race of diminutive people, notably certain tribespeople of equatorial Africa), *midgets* (who are characterized by normal bodily proportions), and *dwarfs* (whose features are disproportionate). William Lindsay Gresham, in his *Monster Midway* (1953, 99), gives this frank characterization:

> Dwarfs are entirely different from midgets, and although medical literature tends to lump both together under the common term "dwarf," midgets resent this classification. An achondroplastic dwarf is the result of some malfunction of the thyroid gland. His head is the size of a normal man's but has a bulging forehead. The nose is usually saddle-shaped and broad. The arms and legs are short and bowed, the fingers and toes of equal length, making hands and feet unusually broad. The spine tends to curve in, causing the abdomen to be prominent. Their voices are of normal timbre, although frequently very deep. In show business, because of their grotesque appearance, dwarfs do clown routines. They are usually intelligent people, warmhearted and generous if they make a successful adjustment to the so-called normal world. Their psychological problem differs from that of the midget. No one ever mistakes a dwarf for

a child, and it seems easier for a man to resign himself to being thought ugly than for him to be considered "cute."

Many dwarfs have flourished not only as circus clowns but as midway stars like Pete Terhurne, whom I proudly came to know in researching my book, *Secrets of the Sideshows* (Nickell 2005, 108–11). Performing as Poobah the Fire-eating Dwarf—for Ward Hall and Christ Christ's traveling "World of Wonders" ten-in-one carnival show—he drummed up crowds by eating fire on the platform outside the show tent. I am able to attest that, torch aside, Pete can light up a midway with just his smile.

Dwarfs at Court

The first dwarf who is known to us by name was Khnumhotou, who lived about 2500 BCE and was "keeper of the pharaoh's wardrobe" (Drimmer 1991, 191). Attila the Hun (406?–453) may have been a dwarf, having had a large head, flat nose, and "a short square body," according to historian Edward Gibbon. However, we do not know how short he was, and Fiedler (1993, 60) sounds a skeptical note, pointing out that Attila reportedly had a court midget, a Moor named Zercon. Fiedler finds it "difficult, though somehow titillating, to imagine a Dwarf ruler with a pet Dwarf."

The dwarfs of sixteenth- and seventeenth-century Europe became increasingly popular as house servants and entertainers. A dwarf who was particularly clever—especially if also a hunchback—might become a court jester (Drimmer 1991, 190, 192; *Encyclopaedia Britannica* 1960, s.v. "Oberon"). Such was the fictional dwarf in Edgar Allan Poe's dark story, "Hop-Frog." (The king of a fabled land kept a jester, a clumsy-gaited dwarf whom he cruelly worked and abused. However, on the pretext of contriving a masquerade, Hop-Frog manages to lure the king and his councilors into adopting the guise of apes with the use of tar and flax. Then he hangs them, chained, from a chandelier and burns them to "a fetid, blackened, hideous and indistinguishable mass.")

On one of my investigative jaunts in Germany, I came upon an intriguing legend of a dwarf court jester at Heidelberg Castle. It is obviously recounted not for its factual value but for its punch line (Nickell 2007, 246–47).

The tale focuses on *Grosses Fass* (i.e., "great cask"), an enormous wine vat standing two stories tall, located in the cellar of Heidelberg castle. At one time the world's largest functioning wine vat, it is said to have been made from one hundred and thirty oak trees and to have a capacity of approximately five thousand gallons. The attendant legend holds that, in the eighteenth century, the vat's guardian was a dwarf, a jester called Perkeo. Perkeo's reputed thirst for wine led to, well, jesting claims that he could consume the cask's contents in a single draught (Perkeo 2005). More reasonably, another source alleges he merely attempted to empty the cask by drinking eighteen bottles daily over a fifty-year span. One day, according to local jokelore, Perkeo substituted a glass of water—by accident, most raconteurs insist—and died instantly (Inowlocki 1999, 70–71; Knight 2002, 303).

Actually, the anecdote may have grown from a proverbial kernel of truth. It seems that under the rule of Carl Phillip, a Tyrolean dwarf did serve as the court jester—like many other clever dwarfs (Nickell 2005, 107). *Perkeo* was supposedly a nickname deriving from his response whenever he was offered wine: "Perché no?" ("Why not?"). Today, an antique statue of the legendary Perkeo stands beside the great cask (Knight 2002, 303; Perkeo 2005).

I encountered another diminutive statue at Austria's *Schloss Moosham* (Moosham Castle), infamous for its many witch trials of the seventeenth century and werewolf scare of the early eighteenth century (Nickell 2008, 7). Carved of marble, the little man was clothed in knee-length pants, a vest, and a coat, and his large head was topped by a cocked hat. He is holding to his eye what resembles a magnifying glass, but I could learn nothing about him from the castle's guide. Was he another jester, or perhaps an even more significant court figure?

The Dwarf Garden

I was scarcely prepared for the poignant set of sculpted dwarfs I encountered elsewhere in Austria, in May 2007. My faithful European guide and fellow skeptical investigator Martin Mahner had told me about the little park where they repose, near *Schloss Mirabell* (Mirabell Castle), as he drove us into Salzburg.

A quiet, tree-shaded little place, it is ringed with a walkway that takes one past fifteen sculptures of dwarfs—here a woodcutter, there a lady fruitseller, a hunchback, and, not surprisingly, a jester. They have the look of real persons with individual personalities, and are dressed in period clothes (see figures 2.1–2.3).

The *Zwerglgarten* ("Dwarf Garden") dates from the time of Prince-

Figures 2.1–2.3. The author explores the "Dwarf Garden" in Salzburg, Austria (author's photographs).

Archbishop Franz Anton Harrach, who reigned from 1709 to 1727). The sculptor is unknown, but the figures are carved of a grainy marble in a type of stylized art, in this instance from the hyper-realistic period following the Renaissance (Steves 2007, 564–65). The prince established the collection with twenty-eight original figures.

Subsequently, however, in the early nineteenth century, Crown Prince Ludwig of Bavaria, succumbing to the superstitions of the time, became worried about the "monstrosities" somehow "marking" his unborn child. According to a widespread belief, monsters were caused by something a woman saw or touched during her pregnancy (DeLys 1989, 219–20). Although Ludwig intended the statues to be destroyed, they were only auctioned off, remaining forgotten for a century or so (Salzburg 2007).

However, in 1921, a beautification group recalled this bit of Salzburg history and persuaded the city fathers to restore the remaining nine figures. Today, fifteen of the original twenty-eight dwarfs repose in the castle park, and there are hopes that the remaining ones will someday be reclaimed at the site (Salzburg 2007). I share the sentiment, finding the Dwarf Garden ideal for contemplating the breadth—and depth—of our humanity.

References

DeLys, Claudia. 1989. *What's So Lucky about a Four-Leaf Clover?* New York: Bell Publishing.

Doyle, Arthur Conan. 1921. *The Coming of the Fairies.* Reprinted; New York: Samuel Weiser, 1979.

Drimmer, Frederick. 1991. *Very Special People: The Struggles, Love, and Triumphs of Human Oddities.* New York: Citadel Press.

Gresham, William Lindsay. 1953. *Monster Midway.* New York: Rinehart.

Guiley, Rosemary Ellen. 1991. *Harper's Encyclopedia of Mystical & Paranormal Experiences.* New York: HarperCollins.

Inowlocki, Tamia, ed. 1999. *Fodor's UpCLOSE Germany.* New York: Fodor's Travel Publications.

Leach, Maria, and Jerome Fried, eds. 1984. *Funk & Wagnalls Standard Dictionary of Folklore, Mythology, and Legend.* New York: Harper & Row.

Nickell, Joe. 1995. *Entities: Angels, Spirits, Demons, and Other Alien Beings.* Amherst, NY: Prometheus Books.

———. 2005. *Secrets of the Sideshows.* Lexington, KY: University Press of Kentucky.

———. 2007. *Adventures in Paranormal Investigation.* Lexington, KY: University Press of Kentucky.

———. 2008. "Werewolves—Or Weren't?" *Skeptical Briefs* 18, no. 1 (March): 6–7, 12.

Perkeo. 2005. http://www.zum.de/Faecher/G/BW/LandesKunde/rhein/hd/schloss/mona/perkeo1.htm(accessed July 28, 2005).

Salzburg Information. 2007. http://www.salzburg.info/soundofmusic_72.htm (accessed May 21, 2007).

Steves, Rick. 2006. *Rick Steves' Germany & Austria 2007*. Emeryville, CA: Avalon Travel Publishing.

Wilson, Sheryl C., and Theodore X. Barber. 1983. "The Fantasy-prone Personality: Implications for Understanding Imagery, Hypnosis, and Parapsychological Phenomena." In *Imagery, Current Theory, Research, and Application*, ed. Anees A. Sheikh, 340–90. New York: Wiley.

Chapter 3

The Real Giants

At the opposite end of the height spectrum are the giants. According to C. J. S. Thompson in his *Mystery and Lore of Monsters* (1968, 129), "In almost every race and people throughout the globe, traditions and legends are to be found of monstrous and gigantic beings who are supposed to live in caves, forests or mountains, to the terror of normal human beings."

Biblical Goliaths

In the Old Testament there are allusions to persons of great stature and even races of giant people. Genesis 6:4, for instance, states: "There were giants in the earth in those days; and also after that, when the sons of God came in unto the daughters of men, and they bare *children* to them, the same *became* mighty men which *were* of old, men of renown." Then there were the *Rephaim* ("Giants"), a giant race that dwelled east of Jordan (Gen. 14:5; Boyd n.d., 237), and the *Emims* ("Terrors"), who were "a people great, and many, and tall, as the Anakims; which also were accounted giants, as the Anakims; but the Mosbites call them Emims" (Deut. 2:10–11; Boyd n.d., 27, 103).

In Bashan (a country also east of Jordan, bordered by Hermon on the north and Gilead on the south), the king, Og, was the last of this race of giants. As stated in the Book of Joshua, "All the Kingdom of Og in

Bashan, which reigned in [the city of] Ashtaroth and in Edrei [the fortress-capital of Bashan], who remained of the remnant of the giants: for these did Moses smite, and cast them out (Joshua 13:12; Boyd n.d., 39, 50, 96).

By far the most famous such figure of the Old Testament was the Philistine champion whose name became synonymous with *giant*. He challenged the Israeli warriors under King Saul to individual combat, but when none of them responded, young David came forth, armed with just a sling, and toppled Goliath with a pebble (1 Samuel 17:1–58). While the King James version records Goliath's height as "six cubits and a span" (about nine feet nine inches), other texts, such as the Dead Sea Scrolls and the Septuagint, state four cubits and a span (approximately six feet nine inches).

The Cardiff Giant

The mythologized biblical giants captured the popular imagination and helped prompt, well, a gigantic hoax, perhaps the best-known one in the United States. "Discovered" October 16, 1869, at Cardiff, New York, was the now infamous "Cardiff Giant" (see figures 3.1 and 3.2). Unearthed by men digging a well on the farm of William C. Newell, it was believed to be an ancient, petrified male colossus or a mysterious statue or a clever fake.

Newell purchased a large tent and attracted hundreds of persons a day, each paying fifty cents to view the naked, anguished-looking, recumbent, over ten-foot-long stone giant. After the colossus was moved to Syracuse, even more people lined up for a look. One was a fossil expert, Dr. John F. Boynton, who pointed out the lack of any precedent for human or animal flesh to be transformed into stone. Boynton and the New York State geologist Professor James Hall, concluded that the figure was a statue. Others disagreed, noting the absence of a pedestal and the peculiarity of a sculpture depicting a reclining figure writhing in agony (Tribble 2009, 167–70).

Finally, it came to the attention of Othaniel C. Marsh, the distinguished paleontologist from Yale. He reported, "It is of very recent origin and a most decided humbug. . . . I am surprised that any scientific observers should not have at once detected the unmistakable evidence against its antiquity." Marsh called attention not only to the polished surfaces of the stone, which belied a lengthy burial, but also to the presence of fresh tool marks. Dr. Boynton revisited the site and agreed with Marsh's findings.

Despite the exposé, the public remained eager to view the giant, and attendance soared when it was exhibited in New York City. Famed showman P. T. Barnum sought to buy the figure, but when he was

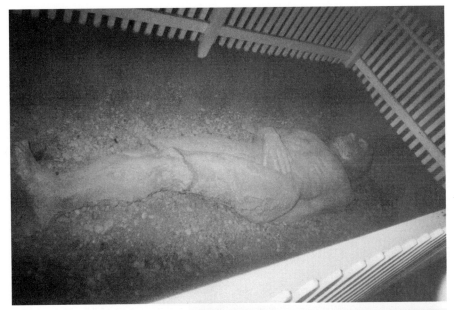

Figures 3.1. and 3.2. "Petrified giant" was unearthed at Cardiff, New York (now displayed at Farmer's Museum, Cooperstown, New York; photographs by the author).

rebuffed, he purchased a plaster copy and displayed it as if it were the genuine stone figure—a hoax of a hoax (Tribble 2009, 167–70).

Meanwhile, the true story emerged. The conception was that of George Hull, a cigar maker and brother-in-law of Cardiff farm owner Newell. Hull had obtained a block of gypsum in Iowa, shipped it to Chicago for carving and artificial "aging" with acid, and then transported it by train to a depot near Binghampton, New York. From there it was hauled to the Newell farm site and buried. A year later, it was uncovered by workmen supposedly hired to dig a well.

Hull said that the idea for the hoax came from an argument he had with a clergyman over the assertion in Genesis, "There were giants in the earth in those days." Hull envisioned a moneymaking spoof involving the creation and burial of such a "giant" in the earth (Stein 1993, 13–14; Kunhardt et al. 1995, 214). (Today, Hull's creation may be viewed at the Farmers' Museum in Cooperstown, New York, where I have examined and photographed it.)

Of Fable and History

Giants have stridden throughout the pages of literature, provoking feelings of wonder and terror. The typical giant of fairy tales is an ogre, like the one in the popular children's tale of Jack the Giant Killer. So, usually, are those of more substantive literary works, including the Cyclops in Homer's *Odyssey*; Grendel, the giant, human-shaped monster in the Old English epic *Beowulf*; Nimrod, the leader of a group of "horrible giants" in Milton's *Paradise Lost*; and even the man-made monster in Mary Shelley's horror classic, *Frankenstein*. Contrasting in mood are such giants of advertising as the fakelore figure Paul Bunyan (who was largely the contrivance of a lumber company executive), and of course, the Jolly Green Giant of canned and frozen vegetable fame (Nickell 2005, 84).

Real giants have a rare condition, gigantism, characterized by overgrowth of the long bones and usually resulting from overactivity of the anterior pituitary gland (often caused by a benign tumor). Following maturity, there may be enlargement of the head, hands, and feet (the result of a syndrome called acromegaly), and still later there may be a coarsening of facial features, with protruding jaws and expanded spacing of the teeth (Nickell 2005, 81–82).

The giants of history were used as soldiers, displayed (since Roman times) in arenas, and stationed as show guards at palace gates, chiefly in England. Such a palace guard was Walter Parsons, who served for King James I. Born in Staffordshire and apprenticed at a young age to a smith, he grew so tall that he reportedly had to stand in a knee-deep hole in the ground to keep him on a level with other workmen. Apparently well over seven feet tall, Parsons found a more appropriate station in life at the tall gates of royal palaces. After James died, Parsons continued as porter to Charles I until his death in about 1628. Reportedly, "if affronted by a man of ordinary stature, he only took him up by the waistband of his breeches and hung him upon one of the hooks in the shambles [butchers' stalls], to be ridicul'd by the people and so went his way" (quoted in Thompson 1968, 144).

The tallest person who ever lived, whose height was unquestionably verified, was American Robert Wadlow (1918–1940), who stood eight feet eleven and a half inches. His parents had tried to give him a normal life. He traveled for a shoe company, using his great height—and size thirty-seven shoes!—to attract crowds. He rationalized he was in advertising, not being exhibited as a freak. He did later make appearances with the Ringling brothers, but only in the center ring and never in the sideshows. Like many giants, Wadlow (who weighed 439 pounds) had leg trouble and walked with a cane. A new brace scraped his ankle, causing an infection that led to his death (Nickell 2005, 89).

Gigantopithecus

In 1934, a young Dutchman named Ralph von Koenigswald, a geologist and paleontologist, was scouring the streets of Hong Kong in search of curiosities. Bernard Heuvelmans, the father of cryptozoology (1972, 94), picks up the story:

> He went into an old-fashioned Chinese chemist's shop. He had come to China to study its fauna, and among the chemist's junk one sometimes came upon stuffed specimens of rare animals, dried insects, shells, or even pieces of fossils. On the counter he noticed a jar full of teeth of all sorts and picked up a handful. It was child's play for him to recognize what animal they belonged to, for teeth, especially those of mammals, are like identity cards to an expert. Suddenly he stopped with a shiver, so astounded, as he later recalled, that his hair actually stood on end. He held in his hand a tooth that looked to be human—he could tell that it was a third lower molar—but a tooth far larger than any man or ape had ever possessed. Its volume was five or six times greater than the corresponding tooth of a man. It was a giant's molar.

The chemist could not say where he had acquired the tooth, which he had had for years. His father and grandfather had frequently found such "dragon's teeth" in area fields.

In time it would be established that a primate genus known as *Gigantopithecus* ("giant ape") had lived in South Asia from the late Miocene epoch (say, 8 million years ago) through the Pleistocene (or until about 150,000 years ago). It existed in two species, *G. giganteus* and *G. blacki*, but no part of the skeleton of either—except jaws and teeth—has ever been discovered. The modern scientific consensus is that Gigantopithecus is "closely related to present-day orangutans" (Daegling 2004, 13–14).

The late cryptozoologist Grover Krantz, professor of anthropology at Washington State University, argued that *Gigantopithecus blacki* had a modern representative, the legendary Bigfoot (or Sasquatch). Krantz passionately believed in the existence of the elusive creature and was anxious to legitimize the quest for it by endowing it with a scientific name.

Unfortunately, Krantz's notion was based on his dubious speculation that missing portions of the fossil jaw's anatomy indicated *Gigantopithecus* walked erect. Moreover, as noted by David J. Daegling in his enviable *Bigfoot Exposed* (2004, 15): "[T]here is no fossil record of Bigfoot in North America. Not one fossil from any time or place on the continent can be attributed to *Gigantopithecus* or any other ape. It did live in China, but we have no evidence that it ever found its way here." Acknowledging that the fossil evidence does provide a "circumstantial case" for Bigfoot, Daegling examines the circumstances:

> The Pleistocene fossil record for mammals in North America is a good one (the Pleistocene epoch included the ice age glaciations in North America and ran from about 1.8 million years ago to 11,000 years ago): we have excellent documentation of a host of extinct forms as well as some which survive to the present day. But we have never pulled a Bigfoot out of the La Brea tar pits in Los Angeles, a site famous for the hundreds of mammalian fossils recovered there. Some Bigfoot experts speculate that Sasquatch was a latecomer to the continent, crossing over the Bering land bridge (a terrestrial corridor joining what is Russia and Alaska today) more or less contemporaneously with the ancestors of Native Americans. Skeletal remains of Native Americans are very spotty the further back one goes, but their numbers do increase as we converge to the present. With Bigfoot, the record does not get better or worse through time because there is no record at all.

We return to the Bigfoot controversy in chapter 6.

References

Boyd, James P. N.d. *Boyd's Bible Dictionary*. Philadelphia: A. J. Holman.

Daegling, David J. 2004. *Bigfoot Exposed*. Walnut Creek, CA: AltaMira Press.

Heuvelmans, Bernard. 1972. *On the Track of Unknown Animals*. Cambridge, MA: MIT Press.

Huyghe, Patrick. 1996. *The Field Guide to Extraterrestrials*. New York: Avon Books.

Nickell, Joe. 1995. *Entities: Angels, Spirits, Demons, and Other Alien Beings*. Amherst, NY: Prometheus Books.

———. 2001. "The Alien Likeness." *Real-Life X-Files: Investigating the Paranormal*. Lexington, KY: University Press of Kentucky, pp. 160–63.

———. 2005. *Secrets of the Sideshows*. Lexington, KY: University Press of Kentucky.

Thompson, C. J. S. 1968. *The Mystery and Lore of Monsters*. New Hyde Park, NY: University Books.

Tribble, Scott. 2009. *A Colossal Hoax: The Giant from Cardiff That Fooled America*. New York: Rowman & Littlefield.

Chapter 4
Wild Men— Or Not

Among the varieties of man-beasts are those unmistakably human examples styled as "wild," as having lived like—or even among—animals. Here we discuss feral children, wild men of the woods, sideshow savages, reputed Neanderthal relicts, and diminutive "Hobbits."

Feral Children

In Roman mythology, Romulus and Remus were children of the god Mars who were thrown into the Tiber by their great uncle, only to be saved from drowning and suckled by a she-wolf. Throughout history there have been reputed real-life "wild children." They appear to have grown up alone in the wilderness or, remarkably, to have been reared by animals (as, in fiction, Rudyard Kipling's Indian boy, Mowgli, who was raised by wolves; and Edgar Rice Burroughs's Tarzan, who was adopted by apes).

The earliest recorded case may be that of a "wolfboy" captured in the Hesse principality of Germany in 1344. But the most famous of the "wild children" was Kaspar Hauser, a teenager in tattered clothes who wandered into Nuremberg, Germany, in 1828. According to *The Encyclopedia of Hoaxes* (Stein 1993, 115), "It is still unknown whether he was an impostor, the illegitimate son of royalty, or merely an abused child." A more modern instance came to light in 1920 when Reverend J. A. L. Singh was intrigued by tales of *manush-baghas*, or "man-beasts," and soon found two wild girls in a wolf's den—or so he claimed. A psychologist named Bruno Bettelheim questioned the story in 1959:

> He argued that Singh's wolf girls were in fact autistic children abandoned by their parents. He based his conclusion on the similarities of behavior in autistic children in his care and the behavior of Amala and Kamala as described by Singh. Bettelheim and others pointed out, plausibly enough, that to observers who already believe they are watching children reared by animals, any animal-like behavior is seized upon as confirmation.

Similar explanations may account for many of the historical cases of wild children (Calkins 1982, 119).

Indeed, sharing the platform of P. T. Barnum's Second American Museum with the Two-Headed Girl (conjoined twins Millie–Christine) were the Wild Australian Children. Called Hoomio and Iola, they were alleged to have been discovered by explorers, who first mistook them for kangaroos. Described as "long, sharp-toothed cannibals," the pair was suspected of being the "link" between humans and the orangutan. However, according to *P. T. Barnum: America's Greatest Showman* (Kunhardt et al. 1995, 209), "The secret that only showmen back then knew was that in truth, the Wild Australian Children were severely retarded microcephalic siblings from Circleville, Ohio."

Wild Men of the Woods

As early as the sixteenth century, in the writings of Aldrovandus (1522–1605), there are found tales of several "wild men of the woods"—actually men and women covered with hair and reportedly discovered inhabiting forests and mountains. Among such creatures Aldrovandus describes are a man and his children from the Canary Islands, with hair all over their bodies. Exhibited as curiosities in Bologna, the family would seem merely to suffer from a genetic disorder. (More on this presently.)

Some of the wild men stories may only describe unkempt, long-haired hermits or deranged people of one type or another. Janet and Colin Bord (1982, 26) provide the following 1885 newspaper account, which offers various interpretations.

Wild Man in the Mountains

Much excitement has been created in the neighborhood of Lebanon, Oregon, recently over the discovery of a wild man in the mountains above that place, who is supposed to be the long lost John Mackentire. About four years ago Mackentire, of Lebanon, while out hunting in the mountains east of Albany with another man, mysteriously disappeared and no definite trace of him has ever yet been found. A few days ago a Mr. Fitzgerald and others, while hunting in the vicinity of the butte known as Bald Peter, situated in the Cascades, several miles above any settlement, saw a man resembling the long-lost man, entirely destitute of clothing, who had grown as hairy as an animal, and was a complete wild man.

He was eating the raw flesh of a deer when first seen, and they approached within a few yards before he saw them and fled. Isaac Banty saw this man in the same locality about two years ago. It is believed by many that the unfortunate man who was lost became deranged and has managed to find means of subsistence while wandering about in the mountains, probably finding shelter in some cave. A party of men is being organized to go in search of the man.

A seventeenth-century example was an Englishman, John Bigg (1629–1696), who renounced worldly possessions and took up residence in a cave near Dinton, Buckhinghamshire. He asked only for leather scraps, which he sewed onto his clothing, including a hat and cape. On his belt he secured three bottles—two for strong beer and one for milk (Sutton 2008).

Bigg was recalled by the 2004 appearance of a "Sutton Wild Man." Dubbed Bark Foot, because his hat and shoes were apparently fashioned from tree bark, he also wore an overcoat woven of reeds and leaves. Described as "a mystery man living wild" in Sutton Park, West Midlands, England, he nevertheless gave his name as Larry Larch and said he was a former "bottle opener designer" who now lived in a tree house he had constructed. His life seems more tragic than mysterious (Sutton 2008).

Sideshow Savages

Then, of course, there was the type of wild man frequently encountered in carnival "freak shows." For example, in 1880 P. T. Barnum exhibited a pair of muscular dwarfs with long hair, billed as the Wild Men of Borneo. Named Waino and Plutano, they were described in their pitch books as "so wild and ferocious . . . they could easily subdue tigers." Their "capture" was portrayed in a chromolithographed advertisement showing armed men netting and caging them. Their act included demonstrations of strength and challenges to men in the audience to fight with the diminutive savages. Actually, they were developmentally disabled brothers from Ohio, named Hiram and Barney Davis, and they continued to be exhibited past the turn of the century (Kunhardt et al. 1995, 270–71).

An 1890s exhibit, the Mexican Wild Man, featured a long-haired man dressed in furs. A circa 1891 photograph by Charles Eisenmann depicts him sitting on a "boulder" and holding up a hand to reveal grotesquely long fingernails. His name was George Stall and he had a successful run, but most of the exhibited wild men and women "were so transient that they changed from month to month" (Bogdan 1990, 260–61).

One type of sideshow wild man was the exceedingly hairy person who (like the Canary Islands family mentioned earlier) had a genetic trait that caused him or her to be covered with hair from head to toe. Such were popular hirsute attractions of nineteenth-century sideshows, including members of Barnum's Sacred Hairy Family of Burmah (see figure 4.1), Jo-Jo the Dog-Faced Boy, and Lionel the Lion-Faced Man. More recently were exhibited Percilla the Monkey Girl (Percilla Bejan, who died in 2001) and the onetime "Wolf Boys," Danny and Larry Gomez, who now perform as trampoline and trapeze artists in a Mexican circus (Nickell 2005, 154–56). Sometimes the alleged oddity was a supposedly preserved but actually gaffed (faked) exhibit, like that shown in figures 4.2 and 4.3.

Another sideshow genre was represented by the geek. This was not today's nerdy person, explains Ricky Jay (1986, 294): "Presented as a wild man, a sort of missing link not truly human, the geek would eat snakes and mice and bite the heads off live chickens and drink their blood." In fact, Jay says, "the act was often faked, relying on trickery for its effects." He adds: "Occasionally a conjurer could entice a *real* or 'glomming' geek, as legitimate counterparts were called, to do the act—usually by providing drink or drugs to the performer."

A sideshow geek was the subject of William Lindsay Gresham's dark study, *Nightmare Alley*. The novel (and subsequent movie) traces the decline of a successful sideshow "mind reader" as he descends into alcoholism and, ultimately, the life of a geek. Transformed by dark grease paint, filthy underwear, a ratty wig, and still more drink, he becomes, states Leslie Fiedler (1993, 345), "a creature disgusting even to his own sodden self," reduced to "gnawing off the heads of chickens for a drink."

A modern version of the wild-man exhibit—perhaps an indication of how low the genre has sunk—is the single-feature sideshow I visited at the

Figure 4.1. A member of the Sacred Hairy Family of Burmah was exhibited by P. T. Barnum (from a nineteenth-century print).

2001 Erie County Fair in western New York. Its signage proclaimed "WILDMAN / He's Still Alive" but "Condemned to a Living Death." Promoted as "An Educational Exhibit," it promised, "See the Horrors of Drug Abuse." Other panels continued the message, with the word "Alive" repeated over and over. A mere 50 cents took one inside to see a swarthy fellow in a fright wig. Chained in a tiny cell, he responded to visitors by flailing and rattling his chains. Humanely, a small electric fan provided the wild man some relief from the hot weather.

Neanderthal Relicts

In March 1994, some spelunkers discovered two human mandibles in a cave in Spain's Asturias Province. Thinking the jawbones could date back

Figures 4.2. and 4.3. Banner art for a "Wolf Boy" exhibit and another exhibit that appeared at the 2007 Erie County Fair (in New York), heralding the actual "gaffed" (faked) exhibit (photographs by the author).

to the Spanish Civil War, the cavers alerted authorities. After local police unearthed approximately one hundred and forty bones, a judge ordered them sent to Madrid, to Spain's forensic pathology center. Following nearly six years of analysis, reported *National Geographic*, the skeletal remains proved not to be those of "our kind of human" but instead came from our nearest prehistoric relatives, Neanderthals (Hall 2008, 38).

From time to time, cryptozoological researchers have attempted to link certain Bigfoot evidence to the Neanderthal period in an attempt to enhance the credibility of the legendary monster's existence. When this happened with some bones discovered in Minnesota, a query went to T. D. Stewart, anthropologist emeritus at the Smithsonian Institution in Washington, DC. Dr. Stewart replied, "the characterization of the Minnesota skeletal find as 'Neanderthaloid' is bosh, just as is Bigfoot" (quoted in Hunter 1993, 13).

Another instance is found in the case of what Sasquatch/Bigfoot author Don Hunter (1993, 103) refers to as "a Neanderthal-type female" who lived on the Black Sea coast in the late nineteenth century and had children by local villagers. However, Hunter admits he lacks any real evidence that the woman was a surviving Neanderthal.

As yet one more example, a Soviet researcher reportedly found a similarity of features between the "hominoid" foot (i.e., shown in certain alleged Bigfoot tracks) and the Neanderthal foot (as reconstructed based on fossils) (Hunter 1993, 167–77). But how credible is the notion that Bigfoot creatures are Neanderthal "relics"?

For some two hundred millennia, the Neanderthals, representing a branch of the human family tree, dominated Eurasia (from about 250,000 to 45,000 years ago), while south of the Mediterranean flourished the species that we recognize as modern humans: *Homo sapiens sapiens* (Cro-Magnon). Many paleoanthropologists suggest that the modern type was more clever and sophisticated, with advanced language skills that aided cultural dominance, in contrast to the thick-boned, beetle-browed Neanderthals, a stout people whose males averaged just five feet and five inches tall. Although some inbreeding may have occurred between the separate species, DNA evidence thus far fails to confirm it (Hall 2008, 40–50).

An overlap between the two species did occur from about 45,000 to 28,000 years ago, but actual contact may have been minimal. One of the Neanderthals' last outposts was a cave in the Rock of Gibraltar, where evidence of their occupation went back 125,000 years, including the remnants of ancient hearths with charred pine nuts and stone scrapers and spearpoints. The most recent of the cave's hearths dates to 28,000 years ago, and its charcoal and accompanying stone tools are the last verified traces of Neanderthal existence. Why the species died out remains an ongoing mystery, but it may have been less the arrival of modern humans than the dramatic climate shifts that came with the ice age (Hall 2008, 51–59). Attempts to link the long-extinct Neanderthals with today's Bigfoot evidence goes beyond genuine mystery into the realm of the imagination.

The "Hobbits"

In 2004, remains of diminutive humans were discovered in a cave on the island of Flores in Indonesia. The tiny skeletons were of a species new to science, that at maturity would have been no taller than a modern three-year-old child.

Dubbed the "Hobbit" (after the little creatures from J. R. R. Tolkein's *Lord of the Rings* books) it was given the scientific name *Homo floresiensis* ("Man of Flores").

The tiny humans lived on Flores about 18,000 years ago, and used sophisticated stone tools. Paleoanthropologists have vigorously disputed their true nature—whether a pathological form of modern human beings or instead an entirely new human species (Wade 2008; Mayell 2004; Krause 2009).

References

Aldrovandus, Ulysses. N.d. Cited in Thompson 1968, p. 99 (below).

Bogdan, Robert. 1990. *Freak Show: Presenting Human Oddities for Fun and Profit*. Chicago, IL: University of Chicago Press.

Bord, Janet, and Colin Bord. 1982. *The Bigfoot Casebook*. Harrisburg, PA: Stackpole Books.

Calkins, Carroll C. 1982. *Mysteries of the Unexplained*. Pleasantville, NY: Reader's Digest Association.

Fiedler, Leslie. 1993. *Freaks: Myths and Images of the Secret Self*. New York: Anchor Books.

Hall, Stephen S. 2008. "Last of the Neanderthals." *National Geographic* (October): 34–59.

Hunter, Don, with René Dahinden. 1993. *Sasquatch/Bigfoot: The Search for North America's Incredible Creature*. Toronto: McClelland & Stewart.

Jay, Ricky. 1986. *Learned Pigs & Fireproof Women: A History of Unique, Eccentric, and Amazing Entertainers*. London: Robert Hale.

Krause, Kenneth W. 2009. "Pathology or Paradigm Shift? Human Evolution, *Ad*

Hominem Science, and the Anomalous Hobbits of Flores." *Skeptical Inquirer* 33, no. 4 (July/August): 31–39.

Kunhardt, Philip B., Jr., et al. 1995. *P. T. Barnum: America's Greatest Showman.* New York: Alfred A. Knopf.

Mayell, Hillary. 2004. "Hobbit-like Human Ancestor Found in Asia." National Geographic (October 27). http://news.nationalgeographic.com/news/2004 (accessed December 26, 2008).

Nickell, Joe. 2005. *Secrets of the Sideshows.* Lexington, KY: University Press of Kentucky.

Stein, Gordon. 1993. *Encyclopedia of Hoaxes.* Detroit, MI: Gale Research.

"Sutton Wild Man." 2004. *Fortean Times*, August 6. http://www/forteantimes .com/strangedays/misc/707/sutton (accessed November 21, 2008).

Thompson, C. J. S. 1968. *The Mystery and Lore of Monsters.* New Hyde Park, NY: University Books.

Wade, Nicholas. 2008. "Fossils Are Fine; A Live Beastie Is Better. *New York Times*, November 23.

Part 2
Hairy Man-Beasts

Chapter 5

Yeti

The Abominable Snowman

For over three centuries, the Sherpa tribespeople who live in the region of the Himalaya Mountains between India and Tibet have expressed belief in a legendary wild man or apelike creature they call the *Yeti*. Because of its reputed foul smell, it eventually became known to Westerners—through explorers and mountaineers—as the Abominable Snowman. According to one source, "He is tangled in a web of fantasy, religion, legend, chicanery, and commercialism." Not surprisingly, "The Yeti is a highly commercial legend, perhaps even Nepal's principal foreign currency earner" (Welfare and Fairley 1980, 14). (See figures 5.1 and 5.2.)

Sightings and Encounters

The Yeti are described as ranging from the height of a normal man up to eight feet tall, being covered with hair, and having a conical head and large feet. The creatures are said to be shy and therefore are seen only rarely and are never captured. Yeti relics, such as a pelt and scalp, when scientifically examined have turned out to come from known animals. Peter Byrne, described as a "colorful" explorer and Yeti seeker, tells how he enticed a monk at an isolated monastery to become intoxicated so Byrne could steal a finger from a mummified "Yeti paw." Tested many years later, it yielded "inconclusive" results but was thought most likely to have been human (Byrne 1994).

55

Figure 5.1. The Abominable Snowman (or Yeti), inspired a
1996 commercial "collectible" (author's collection).

One of the earliest sightings of a "wild man" in the region was made
in 1952 by a Greek photographer named N. A. Tombazi, who only
glimpsed the figure and took no pictures. He said he did not believe in the
"delicious fairy tales" about the Yeti, and years later, he offered a theory
that the "wild man" could have been simply a hermit or an ascetic. As
Daniel Cohen comments in *The Encyclopedia of Monsters* (1982, 6–7):
"There are Buddhist and Hindu ascetics who seek out the desolation of
high places. They can live at altitudes of fifteen thousand feet and can train
themselves to endure cold and other hardships that would kill the average
person." Cohen adds: "They can and do walk about naked or nearly so in
the frigid mountain air. So Tombazi might really have seen a wandering
ascetic, as he first thought."

A 1986 photograph taken by British physicist Anthony Wooldridge
near the India–Tibet border fared no better. Wooldridge and others
believed they were the first to capture the Yeti on photographic film.
Unfortunately, subsequent photo-surveying evidence proved—by the
British physicist's own admission—"beyond a reasonable doubt that what

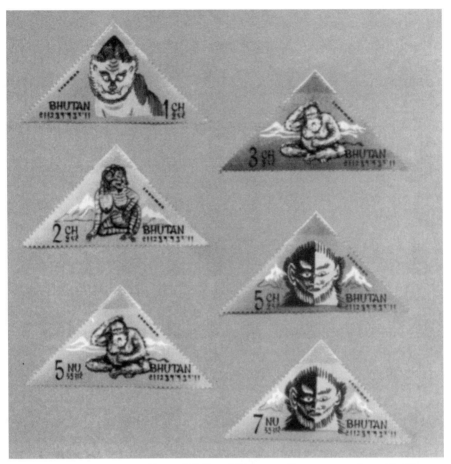

Figure 5.2. Set of "Snowman" stamps was issued by Bhutan, in the eastern Himalayas (author's collection).

I had believed to be a stationary, living creature was, in reality, a rock" (Dennett 1989).

Alleged encounters with Yeti by Nepalese children are intriguing but ultimately no more convincing than Western children's reports of poltergeists or other doubtful or discredited entities. For example, as reported in *Arthur C. Clarke's Mysterious World* (Welfare and Fairley 1980, 15):

> One Sherpa girl, Lakhpa Domani, described an incident to a Peace Corps volunteer, William Weber, who was working in the area of Machherma village in the Everest region. The girl said she was sitting near a stream tending her yaks when she heard a noise and turned round to confront a

huge apelike creature with large eyes and prominent cheekbones. It was covered in black and red-brown hair. It seized her and carried her to the water, but her screams seem to have disconcerted the creature and it dropped her. Then it attacked two of her yaks, killing one with blows, the other by seizing its horns and breaking its neck. The incident was reported to the local police and footprints were found. Weber says: "What motive could there possibly have been for a hoax? My conclusion was that the girl was telling the truth."

However, Weber's view of motives for hoaxes—like similar opinions of other laypersons, as seen throughout history—is naïve: The girl might simply have been looking for attention (Nickell 1995, 224–26).

The Tracks

As in the foregoing case, footprints are the most tangible and most common form of evidence for the Yeti's existence. However, the evidence typically fails to withstand scrutiny.

Consider, for instance, the footprints discovered by Frank Smythe in 1937, which were located in the Bhyundhar Valley. Smythe followed tracks that led to a cave. He gives what Bernard Heuvelmans (1972, 80) terms "a strange description" of the prints: Smythe reported that the footmarks were about twelve to thirteen inches long and six inches wide, but shortened going uphill. He stated that they "were turned outward at about the same angle as a man's," adding, "There were well-defined imprints of five toes, 1 1/2 inches long and 3/4 of an inch broad, unlike human toes, arranged symmetrically. Lastly, there was what appeared to be the impression of a heel with two curious toelike impressions on either side" (quoted in Heuvelmans 1972, 80).

Such footprints gave rise to the Sherpa belief that the Yeti possesses extra toes and walks with its feet pointing backward (as was also said of a race of mountain men in a fourth-century account). Explains Heuvelmans:

Smythe's photographs of the trail showed that it was indisputably a bear's. The marks of the extra toes were really those of the side toes of the hind feet, for when a bear is walking it usually puts its hind feet down in the footprints of its forefeet. Moreover, it turns its feet inward, so that from the position of the prints alone the trail looks as if it is going in the opposite direction. Then the toes are seen to be on the wrong end of the foot, and so the legend of the men with their feet back to front arose.

Another famous case comes from the 1951 Everest Reconnaissance Expedition, when mountaineer Eric Shipton was at 20,000 feet, at the head of the Menlung Glacier. He and a fellow climber came across a giant footprint in the snow, which they photographed up close, and a subsequent trail that they followed along the glacier's edge for approximately a mile.

As it turned out, however, the trail was made by a mountain goat and had nothing to do with the photo of the giant footprint. Explains Napier (1973, 49): "The photograph was taken earlier on the same day and in roughly the same area and was probably the track of a mountain goat; it was certainly not a view of the Yeti track discovered later in the afternoon. The negatives of the trail and the footprint were filed together in the archives of the Mount Everest Foundation and, presumably, this is how the mistake arose."

As to the giant foot track, it was, at only about thirteen inches, "not excessively long, even by human standards," but was extremely wide, some eight inches across the forefoot and about six an a half inches across the heel (Napier 1973, 138). Napier found the foot track interesting but "proof of absolutely nothing" (1973, 141).

Indeed, being able to study the entire field of Shipton's original negative, Napier observed that the footprint had clearly been altered by melting snow. Thus what had been perceived as "the hairy impression of a heel at the 'heel-strike' phase of human walking" was an area where melting—and hence probable "extreme changes in size and outline"—had occurred. "With this observation," concluded Napier, "the footprint loses one of its principal claims to be man-like" (1973, 138–39).

Hillary Expedition

The conqueror of Mount Everest, Sir Edmund Hillary, who died January 11, 2008, was a man of many famous exploits. Less well known was a 1960 paranormal expedition he conducted in the best skeptical tradition.

Born in Auckland, New Zealand, on July 20, 1919, Hillary studied science and mathematics at Auckland University College, later adopting a summer occupation, beekeeping, which allowed him to pursue his winter avocation of mountain climbing. In 1939, he reached the summit of his first major mountain, Mount Olliver in the Southern Alps. In 1953, with Sherpa guide Tenzing Norgay, Hillary conquered the world's tallest peak, Mount Everest, for which he received worldwide acclaim, including knighthood. He subsequently climbed many other mountains, trekked overland to the South Pole (1958), and accompanied astronaut Neil Armstrong in a ski plane that landed at the North Pole (1985). In addition, he devoted much of his life to humanitarian efforts on behalf of the Sherpa people of Nepal (Nickell 2008).

Hillary gave other attention to his beloved Himalaya mountains, including becoming intrigued by persistent reports of the legendary man-beast of the region, the "Abominable Snowman" or Yeti. Hillary resolved to get to the bottom of the mystery. Among the purposes of a 1960–61 expedition financed by *World Book Encyclopedia* to study high-altitude effects on climbers and other aspects of mountaineering, meteorology, and glaciology, Hillary added Yeti-hunting. The expedition included mammologist Marlin Perkins (the late, beloved host of television's *Wild Kingdom*) and various physiologists, zoologists, mountaineers, and journalists. Hillary was determined either to document or to debunk the fabled creature. His team searched the region and reviewed evidence regarding the Yeti's existence.

The investigators came upon what appeared to be fox tracks in shaded snow, but where these led into a sunny area, they had melted and thus become elongated into a semblance of large, human footprints. Hillary realized that this phenomenon of melting and enlarging of tracks—such as those of a bear or a snow leopard—could account for many of the huge "Yeti footprints" that had been photographed. The team analyzed various alleged Yeti relics with consistently negative results. "Yeti fur" turned out to be from the rare Tibetan blue bear, and a "Yeti scalp" was a fur hat made from the goatlike serow.

The results of his investigation led Hillary to conclude that the whole concept of the Yeti was nonsense and that the creature existed only in legend. Monster buffs were angry, but Hillary's prestige and background gave him credibility among scientific-minded people. After all, says Daniel Cohen in his book *Encyclopedia of Monsters* (1982, 9), "Sir Edmund Hillary, the great mountain climber, could hardly be criticized as being an armchair critic."

The Indian Yeti

In India, a reputed version of the Yeti—a ten-foot-tall, apelike creature known as *mande barung* or "forest man"—supposedly put in an appearance in the northeast Indian state of Meghalaya in 2003. For each of three successive days, it was witnessed by a forester. Subsequently, a passionate Yeti buff named Dipu Marak claimed to have retrieved some hairs from the dense jungle area.

The "Yeti hairs" became news five years later, in 2008, when they were obtained by a BBC journalist, Alastair Lawson. He contacted biologist Ian Redmond, an authority in ape conservation, who examined the hairs under high magnification and in comparison with various known animal specimens. He reported, "Under the microscope they look slightly human, slightly like an orangutang and slightly like the hairs brought back by Edmund Hillary." He added: "These hairs remain an enigma. They could be a new species, but the DNA tests will hopefully tell us more" (quoted in AFP 2008). Redmond was referring to the expected results of DNA analysis, that was then being performed by scientists in the United States.

On October 13 the results were in. The "Yeti hairs" proved to be no such thing. DNA tests revealed instead that they came from a species of goat known as the Himalayan Goral, a creature about thirty-seven to fifty-one inches in length with a rough, gray-brown coat. Redmond conceded, "We always knew that the link between the sightings of the Indian Yeti and the finding of the hairs was purely circumstantial."

In summing up the case, Redmond continued, "Nevertheless, the DNA test is an interesting result because the reported location where his sample was collected is way south of the published distribution maps of the Goral species, which is said to live between 1,000 to 4,000 metres up in the Himalayas." He added: "Perhaps we have a more modest discovery—extending the known range of the Goral rather than confirming the existence of the lowland Yeti" (quoted in Lawson 2008).

However, Yeti hunter Dipu Marak was undaunted. "While these results are discouraging, it does not affect my firm conviction that there is a Yeti-like creature out there," he stated. "It has been seen too often for it to be dismissed as nothing more than a myth" (quoted in Lawson 2008).

The Chinese Yeti

Reports of a strange animal found by Chinese trappers and dubbed an "Oriental Yeti" surfaced in early April 2010. Photos depicted the caged creature—discovered in Sichuan province—as it was being sent to Beijing for scientific identification.

Unfortunately, its whitish appearance was its only trait in common with the Yeti. Unlike the Yeti, the Chinese creature is relatively small, four-footed, thick-tailed, decidedly unapelike, and hairless—a condition that scientists believe was due to mange.

Mange (a skin disease caused by a parasitic mite) has long been known to give a mysterious appearance to an ordinary creature—in this instance, apparently a Himalayan weasel, although others suggest a civet or marten. ("Case Closed" 2010)

For example, a "Bigfoot" that my wife, Diana Harris, and I pursued in February 2008 (renting a cabin in the north Pennsylvania forest) turned out to have been, most likely, a black bear with mange. As cryptozoologist Loren Coleman told the *Christian Science Monitor* (April 6, 2010), some of the hairless quadrapeds that have turned up as "Chupacabras" in the United States may simply be dogs, cats, or other animals with mange.

References

AFP. 2008. "British Scientist Hopes for 'Yeti Hair' Breakthrough." Breitbart.com, July 28. http://www.breitbart.com/ (accessed July 29, 2008).

Byrne, Peter. 1994. Interview on television program *Unsolved Mysteries*, aired July 30 (not the original broadcast).

Cohen, Daniel. 1982. *The Encyclopedia of Monsters*. New York: Dodd, Mead.

"Case Closed: Sichuan Mystery Beast Identified, Maybe." 2010. Gochengddoo .com, April 16. http://www.gochengdoo.com/ (accessed April 19, 2010).

Dennett, Michael. 1989. "Abominable Snowman Photo Comes to Rocky End." *Skeptical Inquirer* 13, no. 2 (Winter): 118–19.

Heuvelmans, Bernard. 1972. *On the Track of Unknown Animals*. Cambridge, MA: MIT Press.

Lawson, Alastair. 2008. "'Yeti Hairs' Belong to a Goat." BBC News, October 13. http://news.bbc.co.uk/2/hi/south_asia/7666900.stm (accessed January 31, 2011).

Napier, John. 1973. *Bigfoot: The Yeti and Sasquatch in Myth and Reality*. New York: E. P. Dutton.

Nickell, Joe. 1995. *Entities: Angels, Spirits, Demons, and Other Alien Beings.* Amherst, NY: Prometheus Books.

———. 2008. "Sir Edmund Hillary, Explorer, Skeptic (1919–2008)." *Skeptical Inquirer* 32, no. 3 (May/June): 8.

Welfare, Simon, and John Failey. 1980. *Arthur C. Clarke's Mysterious World.* New York: A & W Visual Library.

Chapter 6

Sasquatch/Bigfoot

Like the Yeti, Sasquatch or "Bigfoot" is described as a large, hairy, apelike creature, equated with the "hairy man" of Native American culture. It supposedly inhabits remote areas of North America, especially West Coast wildernesses from northern California to Alaska.

The Pacific Northwest

Humankind's imagination has always been excited by the possibilities of unknown regions. Thus, a seemingly limitless universe invites speculation about extraterrestrials; the world's largely unexplored oceans and seas, even deep lakes, prompt thoughts of leviathans; similarly, vast wilderness areas of the planet spark belief in other strange creatures, including various man-beasts.

In mid-2006, I was aboard a Center for Inquiry cruise that traveled north from Seattle, Washington, along the coastal reaches of British Columbia and southern Alaska. As part of our floating conference on "Planetary Ethics," I spoke on "Mysterious Entities of the Pacific Northwest," which I specially researched for the cruise. As opportunity presented itself, I was also able to do a bit of on-site investigating related to that topic as we occasionally put into port (Nickell 2007).

Again, for several days in May 2009, investigator Vaughn Rees and I traveled throughout California's Bigfoot country. We stayed one night in a

Figure 6.1. Investigator Vaughn Rees checks a map in the mountains overlooking Bluff Creek, California (photograph by the author).

Figure 6.2. The author drives carefully through a giant redwood while traveling in Bigfoot Country (author's photograph).

Figure 6.3. The Bigfoot Discovery Museum in Felton, California, is devoted to the legendary creature (photograph by the author).

cabin on the Trinity River, and we explored a wilderness area famous for allegedly harboring Bigfoot. To accomplish this we drove some twenty-six miles along a forestry road, then (a road being closed) hiked several more miles (see figure 6.1) to a point overlooking the Bluff Creek site of the famous 1967 filming of Bigfoot (on which, more presently). We also traveled throughout the giant redwood forests by car and on foot (see figure 6.2), visited Bigfoot museums in Willow Creek and Felton (see figure 6.3), examined Bigfoot evidence and representations of the creature in popular culture (such as folk-art Bigfoots), and talked with Bigfoot enthusiasts (see figures 6.4–6.5).

These expeditions encompassed part of the Pacific Northwest, a region loosely including northern California, Washington, Oregon, British Columbia, and southern Alaska. It contains some of the most extensive forests in North America, which, some claim, is home to the fabled

Figure 6.4. The author compares size with the famous Bigfoot statue in Willow Creek, California (author's photograph).

Figure 6.5. Whimsical sign also found in Willow Creek (photograph by the author).

Sasquatch-*cum*-Bigfoot (although sightings of similar creatures are reported in other states and countries as well).

Sasquatch

The name *Sasquatch* is often said to be Native American; actually it was coined by a Canadian schoolteacher, J. W. Burns, in the 1920s. Her Native Coast Salish informants had different names for various unknown hairy giants, the British Columbian version being known as *sokqueatl* or *soss-q'tal*. Burns wanted to invent a single term for all the alleged creatures (Coleman and Clark 1999, 215; Alley 2003, 9). This began a process of homogenization that helped turn various imaginative wild-man concepts into an increasingly uniform type, as we shall see. (I have been investigating this process for many years, just as I did for extraterrestrials, which culminated in my pictorial chart, "Alien Time Line" [see figure 18.1]).

The earliest record of potential Sasquatch footprints is dated 1811, when David Thompson, a trader and explorer, was seeking the mouth of the Columbia River. Crossing the Rockies at what is today Jasper, Alberta, he came upon a mysterious track in the snow. It measured fourteen inches long by eight inches wide and was characterized by four toes with short claw marks, a deeply impressed ball of the foot, and an indistinct heel imprint (Green 1978, 35–37; Hunter 1993, 16–17). Some modern Sasquatch enthusiasts have suggested it was the legendary man-beast, but primate expert John Napier of the Smithsonian Institution was not so sure.

Napier observed that Thompson's description was "an inadequate basis for any far-reaching conclusions" (1973, 74). He argued that the print could well have been that of a bear (whose small inner toe may not have left a mark); Thompson himself thought it likely "the track of a large old grizzled bear" (quoted in Hunter 1993, 17).

Contrastingly, in 1847, a very different type of wild man was reported. Artist Paul Kane was in Washington, in sight of Mount St. Helens volcano, which, the Indians asserted, was "inhabited by a race of beings of a different species, who are cannibals, and whom they hold in great dread." Called *Skoocooms* or "evil genii," however, they appear to have been seen as supernatural rather than natural beings. In any case, Kane did not refer to them as apelike (Hunter 1993, 17–18).

The supposed capture of Sasquatch was reported in the Victoria, British Columbia, *Daily Colonist* on July 4, 1884. Railway men had allegedly captured a hairy "half man, half beast," only four feet seven inches tall and weighing 127 pounds. Dubbed "Jacko," it was allegedly being kept in an area jail but was to be taken to London to be exhibited.

Although some have suggested Jacko could have been an escapee from a touring circus menagerie, it seems more likely he never existed. He was never heard from again, except that a later newspaper article—in the July 9, 1884, *Mainland Guardian*—indicated the story had been a hoax, apparently perpetrated by a reporter for the *Daily Colonist* (Stein 1993, 246–47).

Certainly, hoaxes characterized many Sasquatch reports throughout the next century. A case from 1924 may be one of them. A man named Fred Beck and several fellow prospectors claimed to have shot at several "mountain gorillas" in a canyon near Kelso, Washington. They insisted that that night the creatures bombarded their cabin with rocks and beat upon the door and roof. At daybreak, the attack had ceased and giant footprints were found around the cabin (Bord and Bord 1982, 41–42). However, rumors have since persisted that pranksters living in the vicinity had planted the footprints and thrown the rocks (Daegling 2004, 59–70).

Another case took place in 1930, near Mount St. Helens. Some people who had been picking berries returned to their cars to discover huge, humanlike tracks circling the area. Excitedly, they reported the tracks to nearby forest rangers, but for more than half a century the tracks remained a mystery. Then, in 1982, Rant Mullens, a retired logger who had been working for the US Forest Service at the time the tracks appeared, confessed that he had been involved in faking the giant footprints. As a prank, he had carved from a piece of wood a pair of nine-by-seventeen-inch feet and tromped about the area where the berry pickers' cars were parked (Dennett 1982). Since then, additional footprints and other evidence have appeared, curiously following extensive published descriptions of what genuine Sasquatch/Bigfoot should be like.

The 1950s were a watershed in Sasquatch's history. In 1951, the footprint of a Yeti or "Abominable Snowman" from the Himalayas was photographed by explorer Eric Shipton and received considerable media attention—in California and elsewhere across the United States and even the world.

In 1955, one William Roe claimed to have observed a female Sasquatch for a few minutes at close range. Two years later, Albert Ostman swore that, some thirty-three years earlier, in 1924, he had been prospecting alone near the Toba Inlet, British Columbia, when he was abducted by a male Sasquatch. Ostman claimed he was held captive by a family of the creatures, whom he described in detail, but escaped after almost a week. However, analysis of his story demonstrated that it was more likely the result of imagination than of recollection (Daegling 2004, 31–32, 67–69).

Enter "Bigfoot"

In 1958, Sasquatch was rechristened after making several visits to a road construction site at Bluff Creek in remote northern California. The creature's tracks were discovered by Gerald Crew, a photo of whom, holding up a cast of a giant footprint, was picked up by a wire service and circulated across the country. As a result, "Bigfoot" (whose name first appeared with the Crew photo in the *Humboldt Times* on October 5, 1958) began to proliferate. Decades later, after the death of the Bluff Creek road contractor, Ray Wallace, Wallace's family told the press that he had faked the 1958 tracks, and they even produced pairs of carved feet that matched the Bluff Creek tracks (Daegling 2004, 29, 73; Coleman and Clark 1999, 39).

Another watershed came in October 1967 with "one of the most momentous events in the annals of Bigfoot hunting" (Bord and Bord 1982, 80). Roger Patterson, a longtime Bigfoot enthusiast who had frequently "discovered" the creature's tracks, encountered a man-beast as he and a sidekick rode at Bluff Creek. It spooked the men's horses, but as his mount

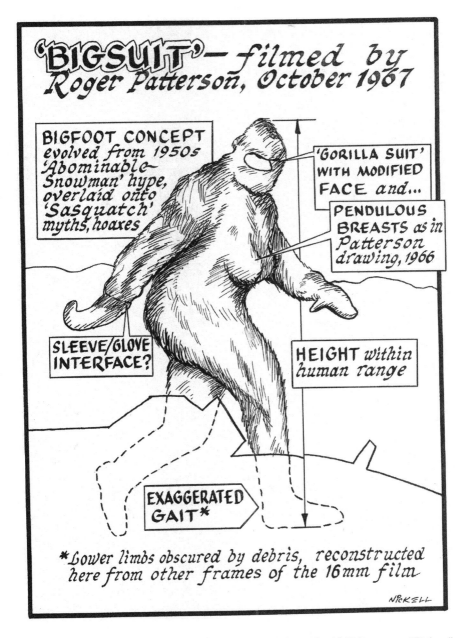

Figure 6.6. Analysis of a frame from the 1967 Patterson "Bigfoot" film shows evidence of fakery (drawing by the author).

fell, Patterson claimed, he jumped clear, grabbed a movie camera from his saddlebag, and filmed the creature as it strode away with a seemingly exaggerated stride, "as if," wrote Daniel Cohen, "a bad actor were trying to simulate a monster's walk" (1982, 17) (see figure 6.6).

Patterson's creature had hairy, pendulous breasts, a detail many thought so convincing that it argued against the film being a hoax. Actually, Patterson had previously made a drawing of just such a supposed female creature that appeared in his book, published the year before (Patterson 1966, 111).

John Napier of the Smithsonian Institution applied his expertise as a primate biologist to the Patterson film, studying it frame by frame and commenting:

1. The walk was consistent in general terms with the bipedal striding gait of modern man, *Homo sapiens.*
2. The cadence of the walk, the general fluidity of body movements and the swing of the arms were to my mind grossly exaggerated. . . .
3. In spite of the heavy, pendulous breasts visible as the creature turned towards the camera, the style of walking was essentially that of a human male.
4. The appearance of a somewhat cone-shaped top to the skull is definitely non-human, but occurs consistently in adult male gorillas and in male orang-utans. The function of the bony crest, which provides the anatomical basis for this appearance, is to give supplementary attachment areas for heavy jaw muscles necessitated by massive jaws and teeth. Essentially it is a male characteristic, only very occasionally seen, to an insignificant extent, in females.
5. The physical build of the creature with its heavy neck, shoulders and chest strongly suggests that the centre of gravity of the body would lie at a higher level in the Sasquatch than it does in man; this in turn would alter the characteristics of the walk, which reduced to its mechanical baseline is a problem of moving the centre of gravity through space. The assumption therefore is made that in spite of the anatomical appearance that argues to the contrary—the centre of gravity of the subject is precisely as it is in modern man.
6. The presence of buttocks, a human hallmark, is at total variance with the ape-like nature of the superstructure. Buttocks, however, are *consistent* with the pattern of the walk and, thus, with the inferred position of the centre of gravity of the body. The upper half of the body bears some resemblance to an ape and the lower half is typically human. It is almost impossible to conceive that such structural hybrids could exist in nature. One half of the animal must be artificial. In view of the walk, it can only be the upper half.

Early in the next millennium a Patterson acquaintance, Bob Heiron-imus, confessed he had been the man in the ape suit (Long 2004), and magician-turned-costume-seller Philip Morris said that in 1967 Patterson had purchased a gorilla suit from him. Morris informs that his suit was made in six pieces: head, body (a back-zippered, fake-fur torso with arms and legs), and a pair of glove hands and latex feet. Patterson may have seen the Morris ad for gorilla suits in *Amusement Business* magazine, says Morris (whom I have talked with on several occasions, and whose lecture on the subject I attended at the Society of American Magicians convention in Buffalo on July 17, 2009). (See figure 6.7.)

Trying to recall events from over thirty-three years before, the man who claims he wore the suit in Patterson's film, Bob Heironimus, described wearing a suit fashioned rather differently from Morris's and smelling like horsehide. Morris notes that his suit—which he positively identifies from the film—was modified. The face mask was replaced, probably by one of leather such as horsehide, and stuffed breasts were added, no doubt from extra fake fur Patterson had asked to be included with his suit. The modifications were necessary to convert a gorilla costume into a more credible Bigfoot suit. Heironimus now concludes Morris indeed made the suit, which Roger Patterson later modified. Family and friends of Heironimus saw the suit in the trunk of Heironimus's mother's Buick in late 1967.

Roger Patterson failed to pay his Bigsuit wearer a promised one thousand dollars, says Heironimus—a credible claim in light of Patterson's repeated theft of services (some seven hundred dollars in long-distance charges to a neighbor's home; about two thousand dollars for printing his 1966 book, *Do Abominable Snowmen of America Really Exist?*; a seven-hundred-dollar loan; and so on and on). Patterson had a habit of ripping people off. Morris says Patterson tried to get him to send the gorilla suit on approval, but Morris demanded payment in

Figure 6.7. Phil Morris (right), shown with part of his "Bigsuit" creation (a modification of his gorilla suit), poses with the author (author's photograph).

advance, and Patterson then sent a money order. Once he had obtained and modified Bigsuit, Roger Patterson was set to perpetrate one of the most audacious hoaxes of the twentieth century. Dr. John Napier seemed to sum up the opinion of many when he quipped, "I could not see the zipper" (1973, 95).

The views of Napier and other skeptics did not convince the late anthropologist Grover Krantz, who believed Patterson's Bigfoot was the surviving *Gigantopithecus* (1992; 1999). Today's arch defender of the authenticity of the filmed creature is D. Jeffrey Meldrum, an associate professor of biological sciences at Idaho State University. A discussion of the myriad complexities involved is given in David J. Daegling's *Bigfoot Exposed: An Anthropologist Examines America's Enduring Legend* (2004, 105–55). If one can read but a single volume on Sasquatch/Bigfoot, Daegling's is the book I recommend.

There have certainly been hoaxes involving persons dressing in realistic fur suits. Just such a hoax occurred near Mission, British Columbia, Canada, on May 1, 1977. Janet and Colin Bord's *Bigfoot Casebook* provides a photograph of the suit, modeled by Bigfoot investigator Dennis Gates. The hoax came only a few months after four Cashton, Wisconsin, youths admitted to a similar stunt. With the help of the others, one of them dressed up as a Bigfoot-type creature and affixed wooden Bigfoot "feet" to his shoes (Bord and Bord 1982, 127–28). Yet another such hoax occurred in 1986 when a Pennsylvania man donned fake fur and a "wolfman" mask and alarmed nighttime drivers by appearing suddenly in their car headlights (Bord and Bord 1989, 32).

A Bigfoot report could cause a wave of hysteria, as occurred after a nine-foot-tall monster with shining eyes was reported in the vicinity of Sister Lakes, Michigan, by a fruit picker named Gordon Brown. As the Bords relate it:

> The day following Gordon Brown's experience, more locals saw it and heard its typical "baby crying" noise, and on 11 June three 13-year-old girls out walking in daylight were confronted by the creature on a lonely road in Silver Creek township. Joyce Smith fainted, and Patsy and Gail Clayton were rooted to the spot with fear. Apparently satisfied with the impression it had made, the monster lumbered off into the bushes. Overnight Sister Lakes changed from a rural community of 500 inhabitants into a teeming tourist center. Hundreds of "hunters" and sensation-seekers flocked into the area, every shop ran a Monster Sale, cafes sold Monster Burgers, the local radio station played Monster Music interrupted by the latest monster reports, and a double-bill horror show

played at the movie house. One shopkeeper advertised a special monster-hunting kit. For $7.95 the keen hunter could buy a light, a net, a baseball bat and, to clinch matters, a mallet and a stake. Teenagers were prone to dress in old fur coats and goof around in public places, but surprisingly no one was hurt, though Sheriff Robert Dool said: "I had to order hunters away because it's getting mighty dangerous; three thousand strangers prowling about at night with guns. . . ." Such circumstances are not likely to produce high-quality reports, since people are keyed up and expect to see Bigfoot. In this state of mind they are very likely to see something which they interpret as Bigfoot but which someone unaffected by the atmosphere realizes is nothing of the sort.

Realistic Footprints

In what may have been one-upmanship by hoaxers, some Bigfoot tracks became increasingly more sophisticated. Consider, for example, a classic series of tracks left in 1969/1970 at Bassburg, Washington, by Bigfoot—or "Clubfoot" as the creature was soon dubbed. The controversial track-ways—consisting of more than a thousand footprints—were ostensibly made by a crippled Sasquatch with a congenitally deformed right foot, what is known as a clubfoot. Grover Krantz said of the knowledge needed to counterfeit the tracks, "This requires an expert anatomist with a very inventive mind, more so than me, and I seriously doubt that any such person exists" (Krantz 1992, 63).

David J. Daegling (2004, 79–87) challenged Krantz's re-creation of the foot's skeletal anatomy from a mere footprint, and he observed that templates for Bigfoot tracks, both normal and deformed, were available in dozens of textbooks. "All a hoaxer had to do was have the wherewithal to scale them up, and he or she did not need to know one iota of anatomy to do so." Daegling concluded (2004, 87):

A footnote to Bossburg is that the form of argument, rather than the force of the evidence itself, maintains the event as legitimate in advocate circles. Krantz's argument as to why the Bossburg prints represent Bigfoot's smoking gun is simply that nobody could have known how to fake those tracks. Krantz opined that Leonardo da Vinci might have had the inge-nuity to dream this up, but he wasn't around in 1969. The logic Krantz used here is not entirely sound. Basically, his thesis is that someone would have to possess such esoteric knowledge of anatomy and biomechanics that it becomes inconceivable that such an individual could fabricate a "correct" deformity from scratch. Yet, construction of a pathologically "correct" footprint requires only imitation, not a career's worth of anatomical training. Krantz's idea, however, continues to be endorsed in Bigfoot circles as the kind of evidence that skeptics have no answer for.

In 1982, oversized footprints, complete with dermal ridges (the ridges that on the hands produce fingerprints), were discovered in Oregon's Blue Mountains, in the Mill Creek watershed. The discovery was made by a new US Forest Service patrolman named Paul Freeman, and the tracks were hailed by Bigfoot enthusiasts as providing startling new proof of the creature's existence. However, investigation at the time by the US Forest Service, and later by noted Bigfoot skeptic Michael Dennett, turned up much evidence that the tracks were bogus, part of an elaborate hoax.

A US Forest Service wildlife biologist named Rodney L. Johnson visited the Mill Creek site the day immediately following the discovery and made important observations. He noted that the pine needles and other fine forest litter had been brushed away before the imprints were made and that the tracks were insufficiently deep for a heavy, Bigfoot-type creature. Johnson further reported that "in several cases, it appeared that the foot may have been rocked from side to side to make the track," and that the "toes on some tracks appeared wider" from one print to another. Also, Johnson noted that dermal ridges were suspiciously clear in areas of the foot that would be expected to be worn and even calloused. Finally, he observed that the stride (indicated by the distance between footprints) "did not change with slope," as would be expected, and that there was "no sign of heel or toe slippage on the steep gradient" (quoted in Dennett 1989, 266–67).

Further evidence soon mounted against the authenticity of the tracks. A professional tracker was brought in but, despite "excellent" observation and an exhaustive search of the vicinity, he noted a lack of any continuity of the trail beyond the immediate impressions. The tracker, Joel Hardin, found that "the tracks appeared and disappeared on the trail with no sign (traces) leading to or away from the area" (quoted in Dennett 1989, 267–68). He concluded that the tracks were a hoax. In addition, Dennett conducted a background investigation on Freeman, discovering that not only did the patrolman have an incredible propensity for discovering Bigfoot tracks and other alleged traces but that he claimed to have had at least two face-to-face encounters with the creature. Astonishingly, Freeman, who reportedly once worked for an orthopedic shoe business, where he could have learned the techniques of making molds of feet, actually admitted to having previously counterfeited Sasquatch footprints.

Dennett commissioned a cobbler to make him a set of "feet" complete with dermal ridges (the cobbler used one of his customers with size-16 feet to produce the model) (1989, 268–71). Dennett then made Mill Creek–like impressions.

Following my Bigfoot expedition mentioned earlier in this chapter, I studied hundreds of recorded Sasquatch/Bigfoot sightings from 1818 to 1980 (in Bord and Bord, 2006, 218–310). What becomes apparent from all this data is the incredible variety of creatures reported (including many that are white, gray-blue, yellow, brown, reddish, black, etc.; that are horned and fanged, or not; that walk on all fours or upright; that have two to six toes; and the like). There seems now to be a trend toward standardization, as the creature evolves into a mythical being—central to a belief shaped by our planetary concerns. (See the appendix.)

Putting aside apparent hoaxes and questionable reports, the fact remains that no credible capture of Sasquatch/Bigfoot has ever been recorded, nor has anyone ever recovered a carcass or even a partial skeleton in the Pacific Northwest or elsewhere. Insists Cohen, "Surely the creatures die." Ah, well, but the *legend* still seems impervious to destruction (1982, 9).

References

Alley, J. Robert. 2003. *Raincoast Sasquatch*. Surry, BC: Hancock House.

Bord, Janet, and Colin Bord. 1982. *The Bigfoot Casebook*. Harrisburg, PA: Stackpole Books.

———. 2006. *Bigfoot Casebook Updated: Sightings and Encounters from 1818 to 2004*. Enumclaw, WA: Pine Winds Press.

———. *Unexplained Mysteries of the 20th Century*. 1989. Chicago, IL: Contemporary Books.

Cohen, Daniel. 1982. *The Encyclopedia of Monsters*. New York: Dodd, Mead.

Coleman, Lore, and Jerome Clark. 1999. *Cryptozoology A to Z*. New York: Fireside.

Daegling, David J. 2004. *Bigfoot Exposed: An Anthropologist Examines America's Enduring Legend*. Walnut Creek, CA: AltaMira Press.

Dennett, Michael. 1982. "Bigfoot Jokester Reveals Punchline—Finally." *Skeptical Inquirer* 7, no. 1 (Fall): 8–9.

———. 1989. "Evidence for Bigfoot? An Investigation of the Mill Creek 'Sasquatch Prints.'" *Skeptical Inquirer* 13, no. 3 (Spring): 264–72.

Green, John. 1978. *Sasquatch: The Apes among Us*. Saanichton, BC: Hancock House.

Hunter, Don, with René Dahinden. 1993. *Sasquatch/Bigfoot: The Search for North America's Incredible Creature*. Toronto: McClelland & Stewart.

Krantz, Grover. 1992. *Big Footprints*. Boulder, CO: Johnson Books.

———. 1999. *Bigfoot Sasquatch: Evidence*. Surrey, BC: Hancock House.

Long, Greg. 2004. *The Making of Bigfoot*. Amherst, NY: Prometheus Books.

Napier, John. 1973. *Bigfoot: The Yeti and Sasquatch in Myth and Reality*. New York: E. P. Dutton.

Nickell, Joe. 1995. *Entities: Angels, Spirits, Demons, and Other Alien Beings*. Amherst, NY: Prometheus Books.

———. 2007. "Mysterious Entities of the Pacific Northwest, Part I." *Skeptical Inquirer* 31, no. 1 (January/February): 20–22, 60.

Patterson, Roger. 1966. *Do Abominable Snowmen of America Really Exist?* Yakima, WA: Franklin Press.

Stein, Gordon, ed. 1993. *Encyclopedia of Hoaxes*. Detroit, MI: Gale Research.

Welfare, Simon, and John Failey. 1980. *Arthur C. Clarke's Mysterious World*. New York: A & W Visual Library.

Chapter 7
Tracking Bigsuit!

I t was, reported a Buffalo television reporter, "quite the hairy situation": In the wilds of nearby Clarence, New York, a furry man-beast put in an appearance (Brason 2006). I was subsequently able to meet professional California-based Bigfoot hunters and join them for nighttime surveillance around the camp they set up at the site.

At Large

The monster flap began on May 31, 2006, on the horse farm of Hans Möbius Sr. (who says he is descended from German mathematician A. F. Möbius, namesake of the *möbius strip*, a surface with a single side). Möbius (See figure 7.1) was clearing brush on his hundred-acre property, in order to begin growing corn for ethanol, and he was taking photos of some ash trees he planned to cut down and sell. He suddenly saw near his little utility farm vehicle a creature that he said looked like a large ape. He quickly snapped three photos (see figures 7.2–7.4) before it headed into the woods "with sort of a loping gait," Möbius said (Young 2006).

Möbius's photographs provoked skepticism far and wide. Stated Buffalo Zoo General Curator, Jerry Aquilina, "Gut reaction is it looks like something in a costume." He was skeptical of everything from the shape of the head, the hands, the color of the fur, and the posture. "Zoologists in general," he said, "especially taxonomists and anthropologists, are usu-

Figure 7.1. Hans Möbius Sr. was a "Bigfoot" eyewitness (photograph by the author).

ally reluctant to believe anything like that exists unless they have a specimen in hand" (quoted in Young 2006). He added that, while a large primate could manage to adapt to the climate of Western New York and survive there, its need to forage for a substantial amount of food would render it unlikely to go undetected for very long.

Jeffrey Meldrum, an assistant professor of biological sciences at Idaho State University, and himself a cryptozoologist (one who studies unknown animals), was even more emphatic. "It's obviously a man in a suit," he said. He noted that the arms were short and not apelike, continuing: "Look at the forearms. There's not a natural taper at the wrist. It looks like a sleeve transitioning into a glove." He added that the hair "looks unnatural. It disperses light like artificial fur would." Meldrum pointed out that the photo series shows the creature in the same spot, moving about, rather than running away. "That raises real questions about the credibility of the photos," he stated. Regarding Möbius, he asked: "Is someone pulling a prank on him? Or is it him having a laugh, just killing time at the others' expense?" (quoted in Becker 2006).

Figures 7.2.–7.4. Snapshots of Bigfoot—or "Bigsuit?"—were made by Hans Möbius Sr. at his Clarence, New York, horse farm (used with permission of Hans Möbius Sr.).

Bigfooters

Much less skeptical was self-styled Bigfoot hunter Tom Biscardi (see figure 7.5), founder of Searching for Bigfoot, of Menlo Park, California. He and his crew of monster buffs (see figure 7.6) drove across the country to check out the story. Their camp attracted a couple of local reporters and me; after having phoned Möbius, I also received an invitation to visit. (I was subsequently interviewed on site for a local television news segment [Nickell 2006a].)

Biscardi showed us a depression in some weeds in a thicket near where the photos had been taken. He had affixed to trees two motion-activated cameras, which, as we got close, took our picture. He had also brought considerable equipment for nighttime monster pursuit—night-vision scopes, a laser heat sensor, a parabolic microphone with recorder, and the like—because he believes Bigfoot is nocturnal (notwithstanding Mr. Möbius's encounter).

At Biscardi's invitation, I joined up with him and his crew, along with volunteers (a couple of young ladies who left notes on his motel door). I was outfitted with a laser heat sensor and, later, a night scope. Biscardi was aggressively promoting the idea of Bigfoot as a reality and he continuously called attention to some sight or sound he found significant.

Figure 7.5. Tom Biscardi, self-styled Bigfoot hunter, exhibits alleged evidence from another dubious case (photograph by the author).

Figure 7.6. Crew member of Searching for Bigfoot is decked out in the latest gear (photograph by the author).

For instance, he pointed to two glow sticks he had set alight back in the trees. He excitedly observed that one or the other would go out of sight momentarily, which, he insisted, meant "something" had passed in front of it. I kept to myself my opinion that the wind was simply moving leaves back and forth in front of the lights.

The Search

We proceeded further to the rear of Mobius's property. Across the fence, from the neighboring farm, Biscardi heard noises he thought could be Bigfoot knocking a stick against a tree, and he responded by knocking on a tree himself with an ax handle; he also broadcast alleged "Bigfoot" vocalizations to the area. I thought the noises I heard were those of frogs, and I was amused when one of the young local volunteers, asked by Biscardi if she had recorded the knocking sounds, replied somewhat uncertainly in the affirmative but added, "lots of frogs" (Nickell 2006b).

Using an infrared scope, Biscardi seemed convinced he was seeing

Figure 7.7. The author explores the site of Möbius's reported encounter (author's photograph).

Figure 7.8. Benjamin Radford photographs tracks—human and animal, but not Bigfoot—near where Tom Biscardi supposedly saw and heard Bigfoot (photograph by the author).

Figure 7.9. Bigsuit puts in an appearance (photograph by the author).

"something"—apparently Bigfoot —darting back and forth before a grove of trees on the neighboring property. I did not see anything unusual with the other infrared scope, and the laser heat sensor registered nothing. I do not know what—if anything—Biscardi saw. He seemed eager to go over to that area but did not because, as he said, he thought the fence was electrified.

I stayed until about 10:30 p.m., then—chilled and tired (I was suffering from a cold)—I left for the night. I returned the following day (see figure 7.7) with *Skeptical Inquirer* managing editor Ben Radford. We had soon climbed the nonelectrical fence and, as I had predicted, saw that the area where Biscardi had supposedly seen and heard Bigfoot was, in fact, a pond. Frogs were making the sounds that were familiar from the previous night, and I remarked to an amused Ben that, if a figure had indeed darted where Biscardi said, it would have had to walk on water.

We carefully searched the area all around the pond. The margins were muddy and had clearly recorded the tracks of cattle, deer, and small mammals, but there was no sign of Bigfoot: neither a track, nor a tuft of hair snagged on trees, nor anything else that could be attributed to the legendary man-beast (see figure 7.8). Later, at the local farmer's market, we encountered a "real" Bigfoot—as carnival showmen would say (i.e., with real fake fur)—although a different type than Möbius photographed. He introduced himself as Bruce Kloc and posed for some photos(see figure 7.9) (Nickell 2006; Radford 2006).

All in all, it seems that it was not Bigfoot but Bigsuit that put in an appearance on the Mobius farm. In the future, I would advise that, before crying wolf (I mean Bigfoot), monster hunters rely less on a combination of hype and fancy equipment and more on critical-thinking skills—unless, of course, their main motive is to get media attention.

References

Becker, Maki. 2006. "Will Clarence Man Have Big Foot in Mouth?" *Buffalo News*, May 31. http://www.buffalonews.com/editorial/20060531/1035858 .asp (accessed June 9, 2006).

Brason, Erika. 2006. "Still Searching for Bigfoot." http://www.WGRZ.com/ includes/tools/print.aspx?story id=38705 (accessed June 12, 2006).

Möbius, Hans. 2006. Interview by the author and signed permission to publish photos, June 9.

Nickell, Joe. 2006a. Interview on WGRZ-TV News, June 9.

———. 2006b. Field notes, June 9–10.

Pierce, Evan Parker. 2006. "Hopeful Hunters Track Bigfoot in the Wilds of Clarence." *Buffalo News*, June 6.

Radford, Ben. 2006. Field notes for June 10, June 12.

Young, Robyn. 2006. "Bigfoot in Clarence?" WGRZ.com, June 1. http://www .WGRZ.com/includes/tools/print.aspx?story id=38464 (accessed June 12, 2006).

Chapter 8
Man-Beasts Range Far

Hairy man-beasts are reported not only in the Himalayas (the Yeti) and in North America (Sasquatch/Bigfoot), but they are alleged to inhabit other remote areas as well. Here we look at several such regional cryptids from Venezuela, Siberia, Australia, India, and elsewhere— although one is a fake from an entirely different place than alleged, as we shall see.

Venezuela: Loys's Ape

From remote regions of South America come occasional reports of human-like apes. For example, there is the strange, controversial photograph of an apelike creature photographed in the 1920s by geologist Francis de Loys. Here are his own words from the *Illustrated London News* (quoted in Welfare and Fairley 1980, 143):

> I was exploring at the time the untrodden forests in the neighborhood of the Tarra River, itself an affluent of the Rio Catatumbo in the Motilones districts of Venezuela and Columbia, and I came across two animals the nature of which was new not only to myself but to the native woodsmen of my party. At a bend of a western minor affluent of the Tarra River these two animals broke upon the exploring party then at rest and, owing to the violence of their attitude had to be met at the point of a rifle. One

of the two was shot dead at very close range; the other one, unfortunately wounded, managed to escape and disappeared into the jungle, the great thickness of which prevented its recovery. The animal shot dead was examined, sat into position on a packing case, measured, and immediately photographed from a distance of 10 ft. Its skin was afterwards removed and its skull and jaws were cleaned and preserved. The hardships met with by the party on their long journey across the forest, however, prevented the final preservation of either the skin or the bones.

At first examination it was found that the specimen was that of an ape of uncommon size, whose features were entirely different from those of the species already known as inhabiting the country.

According to Loys, the creature was 1.5 meters (over five feet) tall and weighed fifty kilograms (over 112 pounds). He added that it was "entirely devoid of any trace of a tail." When a French anthropologist received Loys's report and accompanying photographs—showing the animal seated on a crate and propped up with a stick—he promptly proclaimed it a new species of ape and christened it *Ameranthropoides loysi*. (See Heuvelmans 1972, 183–92).

However, Sir Arthur Keith, a Fellow of the Royal Society, denounced Loys's alleged find as a hoax. Keith found it suspicious that Loys had lost

Figure 8.1. A spider monkey is the probable explanation for "Loy's Ape" (photograph by the author at the African Lion Safari, Ontario, Canada).

the evidence, failed to take appropriate notes of the animal's characteristics, and neglected to photograph the animal with something of known size to indicate scale. "If it was genuine," Sir Arthur said, "there would have been a man in the picture for comparison." It was his view that the creature was simply a large spider monkey (see figure 8.1) with its tail either removed or hidden by the crate. That remains the prevailing view of primate biologists (Welfare and Fairley 1980, 143–44).

Loys's "new species" of ape—like the legendary "wild man," Yeti, and Bigfoot—intrigues us especially because of its supposed kinship with us. For the same reason, certain other notable hoaxes have captured the popular imagination for a time.

Siberia: Frozen Sasquatch

On tour in the mid to late 1960s in Wisconsin, Oklahoma, Illinois, Texas, and other states, a carnival sideshow exhibit featured a remarkable Bigfoot-type creature encased in a block of ice. Viewing it through the ice's foggy surface in 1968, two famous cryptozoologists, Ivan Sanderson and Bernard Heuvelmans, were impressed. Heuvelmans believed the specimen was likely that of a Neanderthal man who had been living fewer than five years before. The figure bore apparent gunshot wounds to the head and chest (Sanderson 1969).

A warning should have arisen from the fact that so sensational a curio had only a most suspicious provenance: It was allegedly owned by an American millionaire who wished to remain anonymous, and he had bought it from a Hong Kong exporter who "offered various stories," admitted Sanderson, "as to the origin of the thing" (1969, 29). In one tale, Russian sealers found it in a block of sea ice floating in the Bering Sea; in another, the discoverers were Japanese whalers who encountered it "somewhere off the coast of Kamchatka," and there were "other versions, but none can be confirmed."

Sanderson dubbed the figure "Bozo"—possibly for a perceived pug-nosed resemblance to the famous clown—and published an account of his study of the "missing link." He included sidebar comments by several leading primatologists and anthropologists but with the proviso that—"until the specimen is x-rayed and properly examined, they cannot, of course, make any more categoric statements at this time" (1969, 29). Heuvelmans had the most to say. "For the first time in history," he gushed, "a fresh corpse of Neanderthal-like man has been found. It means that this form of Hominid, thought to be extinct since prehistoric times, is still living today." He continued:

The long search for rumored live "ape-men" or "missing links" has at last been successful. This was not accomplished by expeditions to faraway places and at great expense, but by the accidental discovery, in this country, of a corpse preserved in ice. The specimen is an adult human-like male, six feet tall, differing from *all* types of modern man by these striking characteristics:

(1) Extreme hairiness;
(2) An apparent shortness of the neck;
(3) A barrel-shaped torso, more rounded than in modern man;
(4) Extremely long arms, which must reach to the knees when hanging;
(5) Disproportionate hands and feet. Hands are eleven inches long and more than seven inches wide. Feet are eight inches wide.
(6) Peculiar relative proportions of both fingers and toes. The thumb is longer than modern man's and the toes are all nearly the same size.

Most of these characteristics agree with what is known of the classic Neanderthalers.

(See figure 8.2.) With continued brashness, Heuvelmans added:

It has been established that:

(1) It cannot be an artificial, entirely manufactured object (it is actually decomposing);
(2) It cannot be a composite, produced by assembling anatomical parts taken from living beings of different species (if the face looks merely unusual, both hands and feet are unknown in any zoological form);
(3) It cannot be a normal individual belonging to any one of the known races of modern man (even the hairiest of the "hairy Ainus" of Japan are not that hairy);
(4) It cannot be an abnormal individual, or freak, belonging to any of the known races of modern man because, in all cases of hypertrichosis, i.e., abnormal development of the hair, the most hairy areas are the outside of the upper head, the chin, cheek, upper lip, axillae [armpits], middle of chest and crotch; here, these areas have a *less* profuse growth of hair.

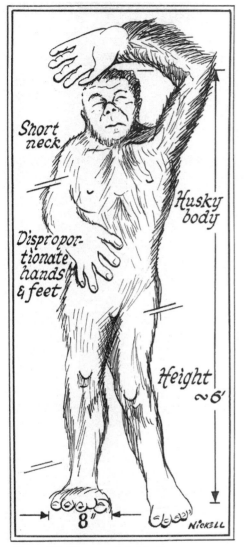

Figure 8.2. "Sasquatch Safely Frozen in Ice" was featured on carnival midways (drawing by the author).

Foolishly, Heuvelmans went beyond scientific rigor to actually name the creature as a new species, *Homo pongoides* (Napier 1973, 99).

Alas, the creature proved to be only a rubber figure, fabricated for sideshow display. It was, in carny parlance, *gaffed* (faked). In an article in the *Skeptical Inquirer* titled "Sasquatchsickle: The Monster, the Model, and the Myth," C. Eugene Emery Jr., a science and medical writer for the *Providence Journal*, got to the bottom of the "mystery." The exhibit was operated by Frank B. Hanson, "a quick-witted Minnesotan" who tried to stall Emery by saying scientists were not permitted to examine the corpse because they would necessarily mutilate it in order to confirm its authenticity. "Apparently," commented Emery, "he never heard of a needle biopsy" (1981–1982, 3).

Emery learned that a retired paleontologist, Leonard C. Bessom Jr., had been approached in the early 1960s and was asked to create a displayable Cro-Magnon-type fake, but he declined. Subsequently, Bessom said, the creature was made by Howard Ball, a top Disneyland model maker—a fact confirmed by Ball's widow and son, Kenneth. "We modeled it after an artist's conception of Cro-

Magnon man and gave it a broken arm and a bashed skull with one eye popped out," said Kenneth Ball. (The hair had been added later.) Referring to Hansen's subsequent claim that he was only exhibiting a copy of the original ice creature, Kenneth Ball said, "This is the original. There was no anonymous millionaire" (quoted in Emery 1981–1982, 3–4).

Heuvelmans's mistaken belief that the figure was decomposing seems easily explained. Sanderson (1969, 28), who gushed that "one look" at the creature was enough to confirm its authenticity, had added brashly, "If nothing else confirmed this, the appalling stench of rotting flesh exuding from a point in the insulation of the coffin would have been enough." Really? That effect could easily have been accomplished by using, for example, an occasional small pour of fish decomposition products.

John Napier concluded that there had only been one iceman. Instead of being switched, the figure had merely been thawed and repositioned. Napier's institution issued a blunt statement: "The Smithsonian Institution . . . is satisfied that the creature is simply a carnival exhibit made of latex rubber and hair. . . . [T]he 'original' model and the present so-called 'substitute' are one and the same" (quoted in Daegling 2004, 78).

In 1973, I viewed the famed exhibit, what carnies call a *single-O* (a one-feature sideshow often exhibited in a trailer). It was billed as "Sasquatch—Safely Frozen in Ice" on the midway of the Canadian National Exhibition (where in 1969 I had worked as a magic pitchman). It lay in a glass-topped, freezerlike coffin. However, if I recall correctly, the freezer unit was out of order; the glass lid was opened (perhaps it had fogged), and the ice had melted somewhat, exposing part of the figure. It was dark and distinctively rubbery (Nickell 1995, 230; 2005, 338). Although Sanderson had dubbed the figure *Bozo*, one may wonder who the real bozos were.

Indeed, speaking of bozos, the brilliant Minnesota iceman hoax was crudely imitated in 2008 by a couple of Georgia men who were soon described as "idiots" and "clowns" ("Has a Real Bigfoot" 2008). The duo, Matthew Whitton and Rick Dyer, claimed to have an eight-foot-tall Bigfoot carcass, killed by a shot from a .30–06 rifle, and—you guessed it— frozen in ice. The men even apparently scammed Bigfoot huckster Tom Biscardi (who had previously claimed to have captured a Bigfoot) and an "investor," who bought the "body" for fifty thousand dollars. It proved to be a Bigfoot costume filled with animal parts. Later, those were replaced with inorganic materials, and the fake sold on eBay for a reputed $250,203 (Wagenseil 2008; Radford 2008).

Australia: The Yowie

Following a skeptic's convention in Sydney, Australia, from November 10 to November 12, 2000—held by the Committee for the Scientific Investigation of Claims of the Paranormal (which bestowed on me there its Distinguished Skeptic Award)—I was able to spend two additional weeks investigating several myths and mysteries (Nickell 2004, 271–334). One of these was the legendary *Yowie*, a Down Under version of Bigfoot.

Like other hairy man-beasts reported around the world, the Yowie has left only meager traces of its supposed existence. It is a fearsome, hairy creature of Aboriginal mythology. Also called *Doolagahl* ("great hairy man"), it is venerated as a sacred being from the time of creation, which the Aborigines call the Dreamtime. An alleged sighting by a hunting party of settlers in 1795 was followed by increased reports from the mountainous regions of New South Wales in the nineteenth century. For example, in 1875 a coal miner exploring in the Blue Mountains west of Sydney reportedly stalked a hairy, apelike animal for a distance before it finally eluded him. Sightings of the Yowie mounted as settlers penetrated the country's vast interior, and Yowie hunter Rex Gilroy notes that his files now "bulge with stories from every state" (1995, 197).

The self-described "'father' of Yowie research," Gilroy boasts the acquisition of some five thousand reports, together with a collection of footprint casts, but he complains of "a lifetime of ridicule from both ignorant laymen and scientists alike" (1995, 202). When Australian skeptic Peter Rodgers and I ventured into the Blue Mountains, we experienced something of the prevalent local skepticism at the information center at Echo Point (in the township of Katoomba). Staffers there were emphatic that the Yowie was a mythical creature pursued by a few fringe enthusiasts. (To them, Yowies exist only as popular toys and chocolate figures marketed by Cadbury.)

Nevertheless, to Gilroy "the Blue Mountains continues to be a hotbed of Yowie man-beast activities—a vast region of hundreds of square miles still containing inaccessible forest regions seldom if ever visited by Europeans." The fabled creatures are known there, he says, as the "Hairy Giants of Katoomba" and also as the "Killer Man-Apes of the Blue Mountains" (Gilroy 1995, 212).

In the Katoomba bushland, Peter and I took the celebrated "steepest incline railway in the world" (built as a coal-mine transport in 1878) down into Jamison Valley. The miserable weather gave added emphasis to the term *rainforest*, through which we "bushwalked" (hiked) west along a trail. We passed some abandoned coal mines, which Peter humorously dubbed "Yowie caves," before eventually retracing our route. We saw no "Hairy Giants of Katoomba" but, to be fair, we encountered little wildlife at all. The ringing notes of the bellbird did herald our visit and announce that we were not alone. (See figures 8.3 and 8.4.)

Resuming our drive, we next stopped at Meadlow Bath, a historic resort area. From the "haunted" Hydro Majestic hotel overlooking the Megalong Valley—also reputed to be Yowie country—we surveyed a countryside that was largely shrouded in fog (Gilroy 1995, 217–18). Proceeding through Blackheath and Victoria Pass (where a bridge is said to be haunted by a female specter [Davis 1998, 95–97]), we continued on to Hartley, then took a narrow, winding road some forty-four kilometers to Jenolan Caves. Gilroy states that the Aborigines believed the caves were used in ancient times as Yowie lairs, and he cites reported sightings and discoveries of footprints in the region (1995, 219). (For millennia the Jenolan area was known to the local Aborigines as *Binoomea*, meaning "holes in the hill." According to legend, the first non-Aborigine to discover the area was a bushranger, an escaped convict named McKeown, who used it as a refuge in the 1830s. Once, after a pursuer had followed him for miles, he disappeared, but his tracks "led up to a wild cavern and into it

Figure 8.3. The author looking for the fabled "Yowies" or "Hairy Giants of Katoomba" (author's photographs by Peter Rodgers).

Figure 8.4. The Australian rainforest is the supposed home of the Yowie (photograph by the author).

Figure 8.5. Terrain of Australia's Bigfoot—the Yowie—is viewed through Carlotta Arch in the Jenolan Caves region (photograph by the author).

... and burst again into open day, and the route lay along a rugged gorge for some three miles" [Bates 2000, 23].)

Except for passing through the Grand Arch, a majestic limestone-cavern entranceway into a hidden valley, and surveying the spectacular grotto called Devil's Coachhouse, we avoided the caves themselves in order to continue our cryptozoological pursuit (see figure 8.5). (This despite the discovery therein of a skeleton of the extinct thylacine, or "Tasmanian Tiger" [*Gregory's* 1999].) We instead searched the surrounding mountainous terrain for signs of the elusive Yowie, again without success. Here and there the raucous laughter of the kookaburra seemed to mock our attempt. Neither did we encounter another claimed paranormal entity—a ghostly lady—when we dined at the "haunted" Jenolan Caves House. An employee told us he had worked at the site for three years without seeing either a Yowie or the inn's resident "ghost," and he indicated that he believed in neither.

Failing to encounter our quarry, we ended our hunt relatively unscathed—soaked, to be sure, and I with a slightly wrenched knee. But consider what might have been: headlines screaming, "Skeptics Mauled by Legendary Beast!"—a tragic way to succeed, certainly, and with no guarantee, even if we survived, that we would be believed! Even Gilroy conceded that "nothing short of actual physical proof—such as fossil or recent skeletal remains or a living specimen—will ever convince the scientific community of the existence of the 'hairy man'" (1995, 202).

That, however, is as it should be: In many instances the touted evidence for Bigfoot-type creatures—mostly alleged sightings and occasional footprints—has been shown to be the product of error or outright deception (Nickell 1995, 222–31). Cryptozoologists risk being thought naïve when they too quickly accept the evidence of man-beast footprints. "Some of these tracks," insists Gilroy, "have been found in virtually inaccessible forest regions by sheer chance and, in my view, must therefore be accepted as authentic yowie footprints" (1995, 224). It seems not to have occurred to the credulous monsterologist that a given "discoverer" might actually be the very hoaxer. Thus, the debate continues.

India's Monkey Man

During May 2001 a mysterious half man, half animal called the Monkey Man reputedly attacked hundreds of people in New Delhi, India's capital.

To understand the phenomenon, we need to consider a mechanism psychologists call contagion—the spreading of an idea, a behavior, or a belief from person to person by means of suggestion—such as the Salem

Figure 8.6.
The lowland gorilla, which was
once reported as a mysterious
man-beast, later gained scientific
recognition (photograph by the
author at the Buffalo Zoo).

witch hysteria of 1692–1693. A modern example occurred in 1978 when a small panda escaped from a zoo in Rotterdam. Following a media alert, some one-hundred panda sightings were reported across the Netherlands. In fact, no one had seen the unfortunate creature, which had been killed by a train near the zoo. Due to contagion, people's expectations led them to misinterpret, say, dogs or other animals as pandas, and some of the reports may have been hoaxes (Van Kampen 1979; Nickell 1995, 43).

In the case of the Monkey Man, my friend and colleague Sanal Edamaruku, along with others at the headquarters of the Indian Rationalist Association, began to investigate. They found that the contagion was fueled by a number of factors, including people seeking attention with self-inflicted wounds, as well as other efforts of pranksters and rumormongers. Soon the police conducted their own investigation—utilizing a team of psychologists and forensic experts—and confirmed the rationalists' findings. When arrests of the troublemakers began to be made, the number of panic calls to the police dropped dramatically (Edamaruku 2001; see also Maiti 2001).

Writing about the mass panic, Sanal Edamaruku concluded:

Spreading with enormous pace and intensity, the monkey-man mania in India's capital has alarmed and shocked us. During these days of hard and hectic work around the clock we felt like firefighters trying to stop an expanding area conflagration. But looking back, I feel that our victory over the flames has not only been a defensive one. The fantastic monkey-man has given us a unique opportunity to touch thousands of people and make them listen to the voice of reason at a moment of greatest receptivity. This lesson in critical thinking, which we have been able to give, may have a lasting impact on many of them. The episode can also be seen as a rationalist crash course on how to handle mass delusions. And last but not least, it has been another chance for us to understand the importance of our work and it has equipped us to face greater challenges and take up greater tasks. (2001, 4)

Others

The foregoing by no means exhaust the regional variants of the type I have designated hairy man-beasts. There are many others. As cryptozoologists frequently point out, although the lowland gorilla (*Gorilla gorilla*, figure 8.6) gained official scientific recognition in 1847, the mountain gorilla (*Gorilla beringa*) first became known by reports of a monster ape that reached Western scientists in 1861. Two of the animals were killed by a Belgian army officer in 1902, and their bodies were recovered for science (Coleman and Clark 1999, 172–73; Heuvelmans 1972, 12–13).

When I was in China as a visiting scholar in October 2010 (as part of an exchange program between China Research Institute for Science Popularization and the Center for Inquiry), one of my excursions was into the cave-pocked mountainous countryside at Zhoukoudian. There, in the 1920s, fossils of *Homo erectus pekinensis*—popularly called "Peking Man"—were discovered. More recently some have wondered whether Peking Man might be a hypothetical living fossil—possibly even the basis for the legendary Yeren, China's version of Bigfoot. Unfortunately, Peking Man (who stood about five feet tall, compatible with the Yeren's reported three-to-nine-feet height) is an unlikely candidate for the Yeren or Bigfoot for reasons including a lack of species distribution (Krantz 1992, 186). Two supposed Yeren shot by a hunter in 1980 turned out to be the rare and endangered golden monkey (Poirier et al. 1983, 37–38).

Among other reputed hairy man-beasts are the *Barmanu* (Pakistan's "Big Hairy One," said to resemble the Minnesota iceman); the so-called "Marked Hominid" (a seven-foot-tall Bigfoot-like creature with two-toned hair patterns, reported from Siberia to the United States); "Momo" (or "Missouri Monster," the Bigfoot-like subject of a scare that terrified rural Missouri folk near the Louisiana border for two weeks in July 1972); the "Skunk Ape" (a chimpanzeelike, but seven-feet-tall and smelly creature of Florida Everglades lore); and others (Coleman and Clark 1999, 28–29, 151–53, 169–70, 224–26). Alas, however, despite the proliferation, not one specimen of any of these has ever been found by science.

There are also smaller reputed creatures like east Africa's *Agogwe* (a small, furry man about four feet tall), the Mongolian *Alma* (a "man-animal" about five feet in stature), Sumatra's *Orang Pendek* (or "wild short man"), and the Himalayan *Teh-lma* (the smallest of several types of Yetis) (Coleman and Clark 1999, 24–28, 189–91, 233–34; Heuvelmans 1972, 64–75). Skeptics have dubbed such creatures "Littlefoot."

References

Bates, Geoff. 2000. "Historic Jenolan Caves." In *Blue Mountains Tourist*, Olympic ed. (citing *Government Gazette*, August 19, 1884).

Binns, Ronald. 1984. *The Loch Ness Mystery Solved*. Amherst, NY: Prometheus Books.

Coleman, Loren, and Jerome Clark. 1999. *Cryptozoology A to Z*. New York: Fireside.

Daegling, David J. 2004. *Bigfoot Exposed: An Anthropologist Examines America's Enduring Legend*. Walnut Creek, CA: AltaMira Press.

Edamaruku, Sanal. 2001. "The 'Monkey Man' in Delhi." *Rationalist International* 72 (May 23): 1–5.

Emery, C. Eugene, Jr. 1981–82. "Sasquatchsickle: The Monster, the Model, and the Myth." *Skeptical Inquirer* 6, no. 2 (Winter): 2–4.

Gilroy, Rex. 1995. *Mysterious Alaska*. Mapleton, QLD, Australia: Nexus Publishing.

Gregory's Blue Mountains in Your Pocket. 1999. 1st ed. Map 238. Marquarie Centre, NSW: Gregory's Publishing.

"Has a Real Bigfoot Finally Been Caught?" 2008. http://www.fayettedailynews .com/article.php?id_news=1832 (accessed July 28, 2008).

Heuvelmans, Bernard. 1972. *On the Trail of Unknown Animals*. Cambridge, MA: MIT Press.

Maiti, Prasenjit. 2001. "India's Monkey Man and the Politics of Mass Hysteria." *Skeptical Inquirer* 25, no. 5 (September/October): 8–9.

Napier, John. 1973. *Bigfoot: The Yeti and Sasquatch in Myth and Reality*. New York: E. P. Dutton.

Nickell, Joe. 1995. *Entities: Angels, Spirits, Demons, and Other Alien Beings.* Amherst, NY: Prometheus Books.

———. 2004. *The Mystery Chronicles: More Real-Life X-Files.* Lexington, KY: University Press of Kentucky.

———. 2005. *Secrets of the Sideshows.* Lexington, KY: University Press of Kentucky.

Poirier, Frank E., Hu Hongxing, and Chung-Min Chen. 1983. "The Evidence for Wildman in Hubei Province, People's Republic of China." *Cryptozoology* 2 (Winter): 25–39.

Radford, Benjamin. 2008. "Georgia Bigfoot Hoax Draws Global Attention." *Skeptical Inquirer* 32, no. 6 (November/December): 5–6.

Sanderson, Ivan T. 1969. "The Missing Link." *Argosy* (May): 23–31.

Van Kampen, Hans. 1979. The case of the lost panda. *Skeptical Inquirer* 4, no. 1 (Fall): 48–50.

Wegenseil, Paul. 2008. "Bigfoot 'Body' Sells for $250,000 on eBay." Fox News, August 18. http://www.foxnews.com/ (accessed October 17, 2008).

Part 3
The Supernaturals

Chapter 9
Werewolves— Or Weren't?

Among those creatures that inhabit the night, or at least the night-mares of the credulous, are vampires, zombies, and werewolves—allegedly supernatural man-beasts.

The term *werewolf* literally means "man-wolf" (from the Old English *wer*, "man," and *wulf*, "wolf") and describes either a human being who has been turned into a wolf by sorcery or one who makes the transforma-tion (whether by will or otherwise) from time to time. In European folk belief, the werewolf preyed on humankind each night but returned to human form at the light of dawn. It could be killed only by being shot with a silver bullet (Leach 1984, ii; King 1991, 114).

Origins

The concept that a human could turn into a wolf seems to have originated with the simple wearing of an animal robe for warmth, with people coming to believe that the man wearing the skin took on the animal's powers. Eventually, the popular imagination conceived of bewitched men who, under the full moon's irresistible power, grew hairy coats, fangs, and claws and otherwise took on the aspect of a beast. The wolf was a popular form of such metamorphoses in Europe.

In fact, there are two medical conditions that undoubtedly helped foster belief in werewolves. One is a disease, a hormonal disorder known

101

as Cushing's Syndrome, which can produce enlargement of the hands and face, together with rapid and copious growth of hair on the latter and an accompanying "acute emotional agitation." According to occult critic Owen Rachleff, "Individuals afflicted with this disease, either because of ostracism or because of the psychotic ramifications of their illness, were, in the past, forced to live apart from society" (1971, 215).

There is also the psychiatric disorder known as lycanthropy (after the Greek *lykanthropos*, "wolf-man"). This is the delusion that one has been transformed into a wolf, which can cause sadistic and even cannibalistic or necrophilic behavior (Stein 1988, 37).

The moon is not a factor (except perhaps a psychological one) in cases of "real" werewolves; however, something of the concept nevertheless survives in the popular notion of "moon madness" (Rachleff 1971, 215). Also known as the lunar effect, it is the supposed influence the moon exerts on people's behavior. As psychologist Terence Hines explains:

> It is especially held that the full moon accentuates or increases the probability of all sorts of odd and troublesome behavior. Suicides, admissions to mental hospitals, arrests for public drunkenness, and crimes of various sorts are all said to increase when the moon is full. It is also widely believed, especially among maternity ward personnel, that more babies are born when the moon is full than during the other phases of the moon. The moon's gravitational influence is usually the mechanism used to explain the alleged effects of the full moon. After all, proponents say, the moon's gravity influences the oceans, which are largely water. Therefore, since the human body contains a great deal of water, the moon's gravity must also influence the human body. This in some unspecified way results in moon madness. But in fact the moon's gravitational influence on the human body is infinitesimal—equivalent to the weight of a single mosquito being added to the weight of a normal individual.

He goes on to note that "gravity is a weak force," and that, in merely holding a book, one is "outpulling the entire planet earth" (Hines 1988, 156–57).

According to Hines, when moon-madness proponents' studies are scrutinized, invariably "methodological or statistical flaws have appeared that invalidate the conclusions," and the overall data on the effect "shows overwhelmingly that the moon's phase has no effect on human behavior" (Hines 1988, 157–58).

It should come as no surprise that lycanthropy is closely associated with vampirism, including a popular belief that one dying under the werewolf's curse was doomed to return as a vampire. In Slavic countries, certain names for werewolves were in time applied to the undead (e.g., *vryko-lakas, volkodlak*). Also, French demonologists described a type of were-wolf, a *loublin*, that haunted cemeteries, digging up and devouring corpses (Bunson 1993, 279–80; Thorne 1999, 72, 91).

Witch Mania

Werewolves were part of the witch craze of the sixteenth and seventeenth centuries, particularly in Europe (see figure 9.1). There, thousands of were-wolf cases were reported from 1520 to 1630 (Bunson 1993, 279).

For example, in France in the early 1500s, three men were put on trial for transforming themselves into werewolves and killing sheep. They were convicted and burned at the stake (Rachleff 1971, 216). Near the end of the century in 1598, a French beggar named Jacques Roulet was also tried as a werewolf. Discovered hiding in the bushes near the mutilated body of a teenage boy, Roulet, half-naked and smeared with blood, admitted to the murder. However, invoking a popular belief of the time, he blamed a magic ointment that he said caused him to become a wolf (whether physically or mentally is unclear). Although he was sentenced to death, on appeal the

Figure 9.1. Werewolf attacks a man
(wood engraving published in Strasbourg, Austria, in 1516).

Parlement of Paris instead committed him to an insane asylum for two years (Stein 1988, 33).

Some have speculated that in such cases belladonna, herbane, aconite root (wolf's bane),* or other potent drugs were included in the "witch ointment." One speculator, Dr. H. J. Norman, concluded, "The chief effect was brought about as the result of the high degree of suggestibility of the individuals, who were undoubtedly in numerous instances psychopathic and mentally deranged" (1966, 291). No doubt even more important in many cases was the effect of torture, which may have caused the accused "werewolf" to acknowledge the use of whatever the inquisitors imagined—ointment or otherwise.

In one instance—the case of Peter Stump (or Stub), who was executed near Cologne in 1590—the catalyst was a "girdle" he supposedly put on and took off, thus transforming himself into a wolf and back. Apparently a serial killer similar to Jeffrey Dahmer, Stump raped, murdered, and even devoured men, women, and children. His was "one of the most famous of all German werewolf trials" (Summers 1966, 253). Revealingly, when his interrogators could not find the magical girdle where the confessed lycanthrope said he had discarded it, they "supposed that it was gone to the devil from whence it came" (quoted in Summers 1966, 259).

Investigating in Austria

While on an investigative tour of Europe in May 2007, I came across a much later werewolf case in Austria. German skeptic Martin Mahner and I toured a supposedly haunted *Schloss Moosham* (i.e., Moosham Castle, figure 9.2), where many witch trials were held. Between 1675 and 1689, when the witch mania had already decreased elsewhere, some two hundred victims (mostly vagabonds) were executed.

The werewolf scare occurred still later, between 1715 and 1717, when an unusual number of cattle and deer were killed by wolves in the Moosham district. When attempts to hunt down and kill the predators failed, superstitious folk concluded that the creatures must have been supernatural. Subsequently, two adolescent beggars admitted under torture in the *Schloss Moosham* dungeon to receiving a black cream from the devil. Had they put the unguent on their bodies, they confessed, they

---

*Aconite, or wolf's bane, is a very poisonous plant, often "added to protection sachets, especially to guard against vampires and werewolves" (Cunningham 2000, 260). It was also placed before windows and doors (Bunson 1993, 283).

would have been transformed immediately into wolves. The implication was that people conspired with the devil to turn into wolves and therefore were responsible for the animal killings. Needless to say, neither the existence of the alleged ointment nor its effect was ever demonstrated.

In this instance, the devil's confessed accomplices escaped execution. They were instead reportedly sentenced to lifelong service as galley slaves on Venetian ships, a punishment described as "a slow but sure death" (Bieberger et al. 2004, 157–62).

Further evidence of the Moosham Castle werewolf case turned up (as director of the Center for Inquiry Libraries Timothy Binga discovered while searching online sources) in an archive of werewolf reports from 1407 to 1720 (Werwolfprozesse 2002). There are two listings for the year 1717 in Moosham: the first, Philipp Ebmer, a beggar, was noted as having died in detention; the second was Ruepp Gell, who, with Hans Pfaendel and five other codefendants, all beggars, ultimately "died in detention" after being sentenced to *Galeerenstrafe*, or "galley-punishment," as mentioned above (Werwolfprozesse 2002).

As a replacement for the death penalty, during *Galeerenstrafe* the condemned man was secured with heavy iron chains to a galley's

Figure 9.2. At Moosham Castle in Austria, witches were tried; and in 1717 men were tortured into confessing involvement in werewolf attacks (photograph by the author).

rudder handle (or tiller). This inhumane punishment typically resulted in death by exhaustion, disease, or shipwreck (Galeerenstrafe 2007).

We like to ascribe such frightening excesses to the magical thinking that pervaded an earlier age, holding our own time as more enlightened. Yet we must acknowledge the surprisingly modern view of lycanthropy found in the sixteenth-century skeptical work, *The Discoverie of Witchcraft*, by Reginald Scot (1584, 58). Challenging the basis of claims that men can be transformed into beasts, Scot sums up:

> To conclude, I saie that the transformations, which these witchmongers doo so rave and rage upon, is (as all the learned sort of physicians affirme) a disease proceeding partlie from melancholie, wherebie manie suppose themselves to be woolves, or such ravening beasts. For *Lycanthropia* is of the ancient physicians called *Lupina melancholia*, or *Lupina insania*. *J. Wierus* declareth verie learnedlie, the cause, the circumstance, and the cure of this disease. I have written the more herein; bicause hereby great princes and potentates, as well as poore women and innocents, have beene defamed and accounted among the number of witches.

Conversely, we must also acknowledge some of the unenlightened thinking of today. Consider, for example, the "animal mutilation" cases that burgeoned in the 1970s and continue to the present. They are often popularly attributed to the "Chupacabra," an imagined Dracula-esque extraterrestrial, despite repeated evidence that the "mutilations" are the work of predators and scavengers (Nickell 2006, 20–21). Perhaps some of us have not advanced so very far after all.

References

Bieberger, Christof, et al. 2004. *Geisterschösser in Osterreich* ("Ghost Castles in Austria"). Vienna: Verlag Carl Ueberreuter. Portions translated for me by Martin Mahner.

Bunson, Matthew. 1993. *The Vampire Encyclopedia*. New York: Gramercy Books.

Cunningham, Scott. 2000. *Cunningham's Encyclopedia of Magic Herbs*. 2nd ed. St. Paul, MN: Llewellyn Publications.

Galeerenstrafe. 2007. From German Wikipedia.org (accessed July 18, 2007).

Hines, Terence. 1988. *Pseudoscience and the Paranormal*. Amherst, NY: Prometheus Books.

King, Francis X. 1991. *Mind & Magic*. London: Crescent.

Leach, Maria, ed. 1984. *Funk & Wagnall's Standard Dictionary of Folklore, Mythology, and Legend*. New York: Harper & Row.

Lorey, Elmar. 2002. "Werwolfprozesse in der Frühen Neuzeit." http://www.elmar-lorey.de/Prozesse.htm (accessed July 13, 2007).

Nickell, Joe. 2006. "Argentina Mysteries." *Skeptical Inquirer* 30, no. 2 (March/April): 19–21.

Norman, H. J. 1966. "Witch Ointments." Appendix to Summers 1966 (below).

Rachleff, Owen. 1971. *The Occult Conceit.* Chicago, IL: Cowles.

Scot, Reginald. 1584. *The Discoverie of Witchcraft.* Reprinted from the 1930 ed.; New York: Dover, 1972, p. 58.

Stein, Gordon. 1988. "Werewolves." *Fate* (January): 30–40.

Summers, Montague. 1966. *The Werewolf.* New York: Bell Publishing.

Thorne, Tony. 1999. *Children of the Night: Of Vampires and Vampirism.* London: Victor Gollancz.

Chapter 10

On the Trail of the Loup-Garou

B elief in lycanthropes (werewolves) long existed in France. Indeed, according to the late English cleric and occult scholar Montague Summers, "the tradition descends unbroken from the very dawn of history" (1966, 217). The superstition caused "particular alarm" during the sixteenth and seventeenth centuries when it became part of the witch mania that ravaged Europe (Bunson 1993, 279; Nickell 2008).

In France, the creature is known as the *loup-garou* ("werewolf"*) but it is also reported in such far-flung New World regions as eastern Canada and Maine, as well as Indiana, Louisiana, and Haiti. How do we explain such clusters of reports, and what are the presumed migratory routes that connect them?

The French Werewolf

Not only is the loup-garou a reputed shape-shifter (changing from human form to that of an animal and back again), but its social function is also extremely variable. Consider, for instance, that it was at times a spectral entity, like the ghost of one twelfth-century count. The man had burned

---

*According to *Merriam-Webster*, the etymology is "Middle French, from Old French *leu garoul*, from *leu* wolf + *garoul* werewolf"—circa 1580. (See http://www.merriam-webster.com/dictionary/loup-garou.)

down an abbey in which his enemies had taken refuge, killing almost three thousand persons. After his own death, he haunted the district in penance, being "seen nightly prowling near the Abbey of Saint-Riquier, a horrible phantom, black and loaded with chains, in the form of a wolf, howling most piteously" (Summers 1966, 219).

At other times, the loup-garou seemed all too real. The sixteenth-century case of Gilles Garnier was among the most famous of all loup-garou trials. Garnier was found guilty of killing and devouring children, for which, in early 1573 at Dole, he was sentenced to be burned alive. Supposedly, he had made a pact with a "spectral man" who had enticed him into his beastly behavior and provided him with a "salve wherewith he anointed himself when he went about to shift his shape" (quoted in Summers 1966, 225–26). In some later cases such convicted serial killers were recognized as insane and treated accordingly.

Another possibility is suggested by Robert Eisler in his *Man into Wolf* (1978, 13). Referring to "outbreaks of endemic lycanthropism," he observes that they occurred "notably in France at the end of the sixteenth and the beginning of the seventeenth century, when rural poachers' gangsterism seems to have hidden behind the werewolf's mask." He likens the outbreak to a modern "native terrorist crime-wave" in the French and Belgian Congo, as well as in Kenya and other African regions, that "operated behind the sinister masquerade of a secret brotherhood of 'leopard-men' disguised in leopard-skins. . . ."

Yet again, the loup-garou was the subject of fictional narratives, such as the medieval romance *Guillaume de Palerme*. In these the werewolf is a relatively benign figure, himself being a victim of sorcery and coming to the aid of knights errant ("Werewolf Fiction" 2008; Summers 1966, 219–22).

Then there were tales of the loup-garou that sound suspiciously like proliferating urban legends of their day, circulating a popular "truth." Several take the form of a story about someone who engages in a struggle with a loup-garou, wounding it in some way. Subsequently, reports the narrative with appropriate punchline, some local person (usually a reputed witch or warlock) is discovered to have the same wound as was given to the loup-garou: a blind eye, a severed ear or hand, or the like (Summers 1966, 225, 228, 238).

In the nineteenth century, the loup-garou seems to have become little more than a bogeyman, as, for example, described by Sabine Baring-Gould: People would not dare to cross a certain plain near Champigni (Vienne) at night because a loup-garou allegedly prowled there, "His tongue hanging out, and his eyes glaring like marsh-fires!" (1865, 1–5).

Beast of Gévaudan

Among the most famous of the loup-garous was one that terrified the folk in the western portion of the Gévaudan district during the years 1764 and 1765. Known as the "Beast of Gévaudan," (see figure 10.1) it began by ripping out the heart of a little girl and progressed to attacks on groups of men. Soldiers and professional hunters were brought in, resulting in the slaying of more than a hundred wolves.

According to the *Paris Gazette*, the beast was "much higher than a wolf . . . and his feet are armed with talons. His hair is reddish, his head large, and the muzzle of it is shaped like that of a greyhound; his ears are small and straight; his breast is wide and gray; his back streaked with black; his large mouth is provided with sharp teeth" (quoted in Clark and Pear 1997, 194). Some speculated that the beast was a warlock, a hyena, or a loup-garou.

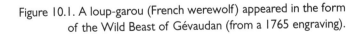

Figure 10.1. A loup-garou (French werewolf) appeared in the form of the Wild Beast of Gévaudan (from a 1765 engraving).

Two different beasts were killed and identified as the prowling monster. The first was claimed on September 21, 1765, by François Antoine, a Lieutenant of the Hunt and bearer of the king's harquebus (a type of matchlock gun). The animal was a large gray wolf that measured 80 centimeters (31 inches) high and 1.7 meters (5.6 feet) long; it weighed 60 kilograms (130 pounds).

Antoine reported officially: "We declare by the present report signed from our hand, we never saw a big wolf that could be compared to this one. Which is why we estimated this could be the fearsome beast that caused so much damage." Further identification came from scars on the beast's body that had been inflicted by those who had defended themselves. The great wolf was stuffed and transported to Versailles. There, the conquering hero displayed his trophy at the court of King Louis XV ("Beast" 2008).

A second beast injured two children in another area on December 2 of the same year. It was reportedly slain on June 19, 1767, by a local hunter named Jean Chastel, although the story is marred by romantic elements: It was claimed that the beast came into sight after Chastel had sat down to pray, that Chastel finished the prayer before shooting the creature, that he shot it directly through the heart, and that he used a silver bullet which he had made. However, the werewolf-slaying bullet was introduced by later novelists, and the other elements may have been folkloric embellishments ("Beast" 2008).

Unfortunately, after the creature's body was paraded around the area, it began to decompose and was reportedly buried somewhere in the countryside (Clark and Pear 1997, 195). As it happened, however, a taxidermist at France's National Museum of Natural History in Paris made an important discovery. He learned that a stuffed specimen—one very much like the creature shot by Chastel—had reposed in the museum's collection from 1766 to 1818, and had been positively identified as a striped hyena (*Hyaena hyaena*) (Coleman and Clark 1999, 33–35).

Eastern Canada

It should come as no surprise that the loup-garou, in one form or another, found its way to the New World—not as a stowaway aboard a French vessel but as a folk belief among the sailors and settlers. In 1534 the French monarch Francis I commissioned Jacques Cartier to establish France's claim to northeastern North America, and New France—modern-day Quebec—resulted. It was captured by the British in 1763, but has remained predominantly French in culture.

After a visit to North America by Samuel de Champlain in 1603, an area named Acadia was also colonized. Consisting of what is today Nova Scotia, Prince Edward Island, and New Brunswick, Acadia provoked contention during the wars between France and England, and under the treaty of Utrecht in 1713, it became English territory. However, in 1755, with war imminent between the two powers and Acadians' sympathies feared to be with France, the majority of residents—thousands of them—were forcibly deported and dispersed among English colonies. (Their tragic story is told by Longfellow's narrative poem, "Evangeline, a Tale of Acadie" [1847].) After peace was finally reached in 1763, about eight hundred of the deportees returned, mostly settling in New Brunswick, and the name Acadia remains current there (Jobb 2005).

In these fertile regions of French-colonized Canada, folktales of the fearsome loup-garou were scattered like seeds. John Robert Columbo, in his *Mysterious Canada* (1988, 85), provides one mid-eighteenth century news story about the loup-garou (because it was written in English, it therefore uses the English term for the creature). It was published in the December 10, 1764, issue of the *Quebec Gazette*:

Intelligence Extraordinary.

Kamouraska, Dec. 2. We learn that a *Ware-Wolfe*, which has roamed through this Province for several Years, and done great Destruction in the District of Quebec, has received several considerable Attacks in the Month of October last, by different Animals, which they had armed and incensed against this Monstre; and especially, the 3d of November following, he received such a furious Blow, from a small lean Beast, that it was thought they were entirely delivered from this fatal Animal, as it some Time after retired into its Hole, to the great Satisfaction of the Public. But they have just learn'd, as the most surest Misfortune, that this Beast is not entirely destroyed, but begins again to show itself, more furious than ever, and makes terrible Hovock wherever it goes. — *Beware then of the Wiles of this malicious Beast, and take good Care of falling into its Claws.*

(Assuming the reality of the report and noting the paucity of details, we might attribute the alarm to one or more predators, wolves perhaps, roaming the wilderness for years and preying occasionally on farm animals.)

As to Acadian loup-garou accounts, there is a dearth of them, attributable to the relative scarcity of print media from the early seventeenth century to the mid-eighteenth century and the subsequent disbursement of the French inhabitants. (Nevertheless, as we shall see later, the loup-garou obviously accompanied them into their southern exile.)

Across the border with Quebec and Acadia, in Maine, stories of the loup-garou have long circulated as part of French and French Canadian folklore. The entity appears to be again shifting its shape—and cultural aspect—this time into a currently popular American man-beast. According to C. J. Stevens in his *The Supernatural Side of Maine* (2002, 220), the loup-garou is "a half man, half beast living in the woods of Eastern Canada and Maine" and is "an entity resembling Bigfoot." Indeed, a local "investigator of the paranormal," a college anthropology student, opines: "I think that the Loup Garoux sightings in Maine are of Bigfoot/Ape type creatures. . . . We live in a world of many mysteries and wonders, so who knows what will be discovered next. For now, the mystery continues" (Gardner 2001).

Vincennes

Returning to the loup-garou's historical trail, we pick it up before the early eighteenth century when French fur traders and pioneers settled the area that is now Vincennes, Indiana. They brought with them their cultural baggage, including stories of the loup-garou. These handed-down tales were recalled by elderly Vincennes residents of French descent in the 1930s and recorded by the Federal Writers' Project (*French* 2008):

> The loup-garou, to most who believed in him, was a fierce werewolf, though in Vincennes, as in New York, the loup-garou may also be a person transformed into a cow, horse, or some other animal. Once under a spell as a loup-garou, the unfortunate victim became an enraged animal that roamed each night through the fields and forests for a certain period of time, usually 101 days. During the day, he returned to his human form, though he was continually morose and sickly and fearful to tell of his predicament lest even a worse sentence should befall. The main way he could be released from the spell before serving the stipulated time was for someone to recognize him as a person transformed to an animal and somehow draw blood from the loup-garou. Even when the disenchantment had been performed, both the victim and his rescuer could not mention the incident, even to each other, until the time was up. Anyone who

violated this tabu would become possessed immediately and face a much stiffer sentence.

Some additional loup-garou and other supernatural folktales were collected in the 1920s and include narratives like "Jean Baptiste Loup-Garou Horse," "Charlie Page's Loup-Garou Story," and "The Loup-Garou Cow" ("Loup-Garou" 2008).

Louisiana

When the French Acadians were deported in 1755 and dispersed among English colonies, one group made its way to Louisiana, to Bayou Teche. The French Louisianans of Acadian descent became known as Cajuns (a corruption of *Acadians*).

The Cajuns joined other French settlers in Louisiana. Robert Cavelier had ventured down the Mississippi in 1862 and claimed the area for France (naming it in honor of Louis XIV). The first settlement was a fort built in 1699. More immigrants followed the founding of New Orleans in 1717, with several ships arriving over the next two years.

Notwithstanding the fakeloric "vampire" hype of New Orleans (based on the fictions of writer Anne Rice rather than on authentic folk traditions), there is a rich cache of loup-garou lore in Louisiana. Observes local writer Victor C. Klein (1999, 109): "Apart from the legends of Native Americans, traditions of Vampires and Werewolves are basically absent from European–American mythology. The general exception to the reality is the belief in the Loup-Garous (pronounced Roo-Ga-Roo) by Cajuns and the Creole Afro-American populations of southern Louisiana."

When the notorious voodoo priestess Marie Laveau (1801–1881) presided over the annual ritual of St. John's Eve in New Orleans, she included the loup-garou in her ceremonies. With drum beating, bonfires, animal sacrifice, and other elements—including nude women dancing seductively—the ritual also featured offerings made to the appropriate *loas* (supernatural entities) for protection. This included safeguarding children and others from the loup-garou, who among the Cajuns is a sort of bogeyman said to feed on the blood of victims (Gandolfo 1992, 18–23).

Louisiana writers Lyle Saxon and Robert Tallant (1945, 191) capture the cultural shape-shifting of the Cajuns' loup-garou:

> There are many "loup-garous," some, people under a spell, and others enjoying self-imposed enchantment. A Cajun will explain: "Loup-garous

is them people what wants to do bad work, and changes themselves into wolves. They got plenty of them, yes. And you sure know them when you see them. They got big red eyes, pointed noses and everything just like a wolf has, even hair all over, and long pointed nails. They rub themselves with some Voo-Doo grease and come out just like wolves is. You keep away you see any of them things, hein? They make you one of them, yes, quick like hell. They hold balls on Bayou Goula all the time, mens and womens, them. If you see one, you just get yourself one nice frog and throw him at them things. They sure gon' run then. They scared of frogs. That's the only way to chase a "loup-garou" away from you. Bullets go right through them.

They continue:

"Loup-garous" have bats as big as airplanes to carry them where they want to go. They make these bats drop them down your chimney, and they stand by your bed and say, "I got you now, me!" Then they bite you and suck your blood and that makes you a "loup-garou," and soon you find yourself dancing at their balls at Bayou Goula and carrying on just as they do. You're a lost soul.

A Cajun advises: "Is a good idea to hang a new sifter outside from your house, yes. Then they got to stop and count every home in that sifter, and you catch them and sprinkle them with salt. That sets them on fire and they step out of them shaggy old skins and runs away. But me, I don't fool 'round with no loup-garous!" (quoted in Saxon and Tallant 1945, 191). Another Cajun, Jerome Dupré, who hunts alligators in the swamps, sees the loup-garou as among the most dangerous of entities. In his lyrical Cajun speech (wherein *loup-garou* becomes a melodious *rougarou*) he describes the creature as devilish and shape-shifting. He says his parents warned him as a child: "If you gonna go to Grandma's house, now you stay on that path. Now don't you step off that path because if you go out there to pick yourself a pretty flower, it can be a *rougarou*. And the *rougarou* is gonna change himself. He's gonna bite you on the neck, and you're gonna spend the rest of your life dancing with the other werewolves on Bayou Goula" (Sillery 2001, 102).

In some Cajun lore, however, the creature is not indiscriminately predatory but rather sort of an avenging angel. Among the predominantly Roman Catholic Cajuns, it is said that the "Rougarou" will "hunt down and kill Catholics that do not follow the rules of Lent"—an interesting concept for a werewolf indeed! Moreover, "In some Cajun communities the Loup Garou of legend have taken on an almost protective role. Children are warned that Loup Garou can read souls, and that they only hunt and kill evil men and unbehaved horses" ("Cajun" 2008).

Some children see the loup-garou while lying abed—clearly experiencing what psychologists and neurologists call "waking dreams." These occur in the twilight between wakefulness and sleep and are responsible for many other bedside entities (Nickell 1995, 41, 44, 117). Reports one Cajun woman: "My mama used to tell me that if I didn't behave myself, she'd sic the loup-garou on me. That was what we called these things. One night, when I had been particularly bad, she did. A loup-garou came and stood at the foot of my bed. I was a really good girl after that—at least for a while" ("Monsters" 2008).

Haiti

Southeast of Louisiana, in the West Indies, French-settled Haiti is another lair for the creature. There, the *loogaroo* is a sort of witch–vampire, a human, typically an old hag, who has formed a pact with the devil. She thereby obtains magical powers so long as she makes offerings of victims' blood. Nightly, the loogaroo visits the Devil Tree (the silk-cotton tree) where she removes her skin, neatly folding and hiding it. Then she soars into homes, unimpeded by windows or doors, and drinks the blood of the sleeping inhabitants. As a protection (evoking some Cajun motifs), one may scatter sand and rice outside the house, which forces the loogaroo to halt and gather each grain. Since this takes hours, before the task is completed, dawn arrives, rendering the loogaroo "visible to one and all, its disguise abandoned." Should a loogaroo's skin be discovered at night, salt may be sprinkled on it, preventing the creature from returning to it and so being exposed at dawn (Bunson 1993, 162–63).

Vampirologist Tony Thorne in his *Children of the Night: Of Vampires and Vampirism* (1999, 118), says of the Haitian creature: "Like the European werewolves and Vampires it was viewed as shifting between the human, animal and supernatural worlds." He adds: "The expert consensus is that the *Loo-garou* is the product of a fearfully poorer-than-poor community whose integrity is so precarious that people have come to be mortally afraid of the outside world, even of their nearest neighbors."

In its many forms and roles—whether as phantom or human predator, magical protector or devil's agent, metamorphosing manimal or versatile shape-shifter, subject of literary romance or vampiric bogeyman—we find the loup-garou inhabiting far-flung locales. We see that early French émigrés carried the concept abroad and thence from place to place, in each of which it was further transformed, providing clear evidence of the cultural rather than factual basis for the belief.

References

Baring-Gould, Sabine. 1865. *The Book of Were-Wolves*. Cited in Summers 1966, p. 238 (below).

"Beast of Gévaudan." 2008. Wikipedia. http://en.wikipedia.org/wiki/Beast_of _G%C3%A9vaudan (accessed November 20, 2008).

Bunson, Matthew. 1993. *The Vampire Encyclopedia*. New York: Grammercy Books.

"Cajun." 2008. Wikipedia. http://enwikipedia.org/wiki/Cajun (accessed July 24, 2008).

Coleman, Loren, and Jerome Clark. 1999. *Cryptozoology A to Z*. New York: Fireside.

Clark, Jerome, and Nancy Pear. 1997. *Strange & Unexplained Phenomena*. New York: Visible Ink.

Colombo, John Robert. 1988. *Mysterious Canada: Strange Sights, Extraordinary Events, and Peculiar Places*. Toronto: Doubleday Canada Limited.

Eisler, Robert. 1978. *Man into Wolf: An Anthropological Interpretation of Sadism, Masochism, and Lycanthropy*. Santa Barbara, CA: Ross-Erikson.

Encyclopedia Britannica. 1960. Chicago, IL: Encyclopedia Britannica.

French Folklife in Old Vincennes. 1989. Terre Haute: Indian Council of Teachers of English, Hoosier Folklore Society. Cited in "Loup-Garou" 2008 (below).

Gandolfo, Charles. 1992. *Marie Laveau of New Orleans*. New Orleans, LA: New Orleans Historic Voodoo Museum.

Gardner, Christopher. 2001. Quoted in Stevens 2002, p. 222 (below).

Jobb, Dean. 2005. *The Acadians: A People's Story of Exile and Triumph*. Mississauga, ON: John Wiley & Sons Canada.

Klein, Victor. 1999. *New Orleans Ghosts II*. Metaire, LA: Lycanthrope Press.

Longfellow, Henry Wadsworth. 1847. "Evangeline: A Tale of Acadie." In *Favorite Poems of Henry Wadsworth Longfellow*. Garden City, NY: Doubleday & Co., 1947, pp. 316–62.

"The Loup-Garou Legends of Old Vincennes." 2008. http://rking.vinu.edu/ loup.htm (accessed July 24, 2008).

"Monsters Haunt Cajun Folk Tales." 2008. http://farshores.org/c07wwolf.htm (accessed July 25, 2008).

Nickell, Joe. 1995. *Entities: Angels, Spirits, Demons, and Other Alien Beings.* Amherst, NY: Prometheus Books.

———. 2008. "Werewolves—Or Weren't?" *Skeptical Briefs* 18, no. 1 (March): 6–7, 12.

Saxon, Lyle, and Robert Tallant. 1945. *Gumbo Va-Va.* Louisiana Writers Project Publishers, 3rd series. Cambridge, MA: Riverside Press. Quoted in Klein 1999, pp. 109–10 (above).

Sillery, Barbara. 2001. *The Haunting of Louisiana.* Gretna, LA: Pelican Publishing.

Stevens, C. J. 2002. *The Supernatural Side of Maine.* Phillips, ME: John Wade.

Summers, Montague. 1966. *The Werewolf.* New York: Bell Publishing.

Thorne, Tony. 1999. *Children of the Night: Of Vampires and Vampirism.* London: Victor Gollancz.

"Werewolf Fiction." 2008. Wikipedia. http://en.wikipedia.org/wiki/Werewolf _fiction (accessed July 24, 2008).

Chapter II
Of Vampirology

Perhaps the quintessential horrific creature of the night is the vampire, "a living corpse or soulless body that comes from its burial place and drinks the blood of the living" (Leach 1984, 1154). Although it is typically a Slavic concept—hence the setting of Bram Stoker's classic, *Dracula* (1897), in Romania—belief in vampires is found in many cultures (Bunson 2000).

The Undead

Tales of the "living dead" can be traced back to ancient Greece, where mythological creatures flourished. For example, Empusa, a daughter of the goddess Hecate, was a demonic being who transformed herself into a beautiful young maiden to seduce men in their sleep, and Lamia was a monster that lived on children's flesh and blood. However there is no direct connection between these mythological beings and today's vampire.

From eleventh-century Europe came stories of corpses seen roaming beyond their tombs or discovered intact in their coffins. This type of living dead became known as *cadaver sanguisugus*, a Latin term meaning "bloodsucking corpse." By the fourteenth century, belief in vampirism became endemic in central Europe (in Prussia, Silesia, and Bohemia), coincident with outbreaks there of bubonic plague (Marigny 1994, 16, 23–24). Indeed vampirism has often been linked to plagues, with the initial victim being thought one of the undead. By exhuming, staking, and burning the initial vampire's corpse, it was thought, subsequent victims would be quieted in their graves, so ending the epidemic (Bunson 2000, 200–201).

Ironically, Christianity—the avowed opponent of everything evil, including vampires—helped to shape European belief in the concept. As it did with witchcraft, the Catholic Church treated vampirism as real. The Church's anti-witch doctrine *Malleus Maleficarum* (or "witch hammer"), issued in 1485, declared that the devil made use of corpses to assail humankind. "In this tradition," states Matthew Bunson in *The Vampire Encyclopedia*, "and derived from the rapidly growing legends or customs of the dead, learned theologians authored pseudoscientific treatises, collecting hearsay, doctrine and often pure fantasy into lengthy works that came to be accepted as fact." "Church leaders," he continues, "having fostered widespread hysteria, were seemingly the only officials capable of dealing with the crisis as terrified villagers turned to clerics to serve as their vampire hunters" (2000, 47).

Dracula et al.

Vampires became the stuff of gothic horror tales with the 1819 publication of "The Vampyre" by John Polidori, followed by others, most notably Bram Stoker's classic, *Dracula*, in 1897. As is well known, Stoker's Count Dracula is very loosely based on the Romanian Vlad Tepes (Polidoro 2006). As popular occult writers Colin Wilson and Damon Wilson explain (1992, 372–73):

> For more than four centuries the Turks had dominated Eastern Europe, marching in and out of Transylvania, Walachia, and Hungary and even conquering Constantinople in 1453. Don John of Austria defeated them at the great sea battle of Lepanto (1571), but it was their failure to capture Vienna after a siege in 1683 that caused the breakup of the Ottoman Empire. During the earlier stages of this war between Europe and Turkey, the man whose name has become synonymous with vampirism—Dracula, or Vlad the Impaler—struck blow after blow against the Turks, until they killed and beheaded him in 1477.
>
> Vlad Tepes (the Impaler), king of Walachia (1456–62, 1476–77), was, as his nickname implies, a man of sadistic temperament, whose greatest pleasure was to impale his enemies (which meant anyone against whom he had a grudge) on pointed stakes; the stake—driven into the ground—was inserted into the anus (or, in the case of women, the

vagina), and the victim was allowed to impale himself slowly under his own weight. . . . In his own time he was known as Dracula, which means "son of a dragon" or "son of the Devil." It is estimated that Dracula had about one hundred thousand people impaled during the course of a lifetime. When he conquered Brasov, in Transylvania, he had all its inhabitants impaled on poles, then gave a feast among the corpses. When one nobleman held his nose at the stench, Vlad sent for a particularly long pole and had him impaled. When he was a prisoner in Hungary, Vlad was kept supplied with birds, rats, and toads, which he impaled on small stakes. A brave and fearless warrior, he was finally killed in battle—or possibly assassinated by his own soldiers—and his head sent to Constantinople. Four hundred twenty years later, in 1897, he was immortalized by Bram Stoker as the sinister Count Dracula, no longer a sadistic maniac, but a drinker of blood.

Over time, vampires have evolved in the popular imagination into a variety of often-conflicting concepts. Are they, as some would suggest, demons, or ghosts, or aliens? Are they living people? Can one be born a vampire? According to vampirologist Jay Stevenson (2002, 29–30):

> The short answer to these questions is that the familiar mainstream vampire inherited from Slavic legend and popularized in books and movies is the undead, reanimated corpse of a former human being—not born that way, not from planet Drakulon, not simply alive, nor a ghost, nor a demon. In general, this traditional undead vampire has awakened the most interest, attention, and terror.

However,

> The longer answer is that vampire lore is living mythology. People continue to use the vampire concept in new ways, combining it with new ideas and incorporating it into new realities. So to really understand vampires, it helps to see them in various contexts, not just stomping around the Transylvanian castle or sleeping in the coffin that opens from the inside.

"Real" Vampires

In addition to myths, plagues, church, doctrine, and literature, the concept of vampirism is indebted to other factors. These include the disease known as *hemothymia* (characterized by a bizarre craving for blood), the South

American vampire bat (which siphons blood from sleeping victims, usually animals), premature burials (especially due to hasty interments necessitated by plague), and "waking dreams." These occur in the interface between sleep and wakefulness and thus are characterized by fantasy elements perceived as real. Such an experience may be accompanied by "sleep paralysis" (so called because the body is still in the sleep mode)—hence the reports of people waking to find a vampire lying upon them (Rachleff 1871, 214–15; Robbins 1959, 521–25; Bunson 2000, 211; Nickell 1995, 41, 117).

Despite such clear explanations for vampire delusions, occultists still like to suggest that vampires might really exist. Wilson and Wilson cite the story of an eighteenth-century Serbian man, Peter Plogojowitz, whose body was exhumed and, except for a somewhat sunken nose, "was completely fresh" and even had "some fresh blood in his mouth" (1992, 374–76). However, just such characteristics are frequently said to describe the "incorruptible" bodies of saints, for example, that of St. Sperandia (1216–1276), which was found intact well after her burial and exuded a "blood-fluid" (Cruz 1977, 48). Roman Catholics would not appreciate the suggestion that their saints were actually vampires! In contrast to the corpse of St. Sperandia, which was exhumed two years after her death, that of Plogojowitz had been interred little more than ten weeks.

Actually, bodies occasionally are found "incorruptible"—not only those said to be vampires or saints but also ordinary people—due to a variety of reasons. These include being kept in sandy soil or in a dry tomb and catacombs, which promotes dessication—i.e., mummification—or, alternately, being submerged in water or wet soil, which can change the fatty tissue into a soaplike substance called *adipocere*, known popularly as "grave wax" (Nickell 2001, 4–9).

The claim that Plogojowitz was a vampire supposedly came from nine people who had died following a one-day illness and who "said publicly," according to an account of 1725, "while they were yet alive, but on their deathbed, that the above-mentioned Peter Plogojowitz, who had died ten weeks earlier, had come to them in their sleep, laid himself on them, and throttled them, so that they would have to give up the ghost" (quoted in Wilson and Wilson 1992, 375). In fact, the evidence suggests that the villagers died of a plague, that Plogojowitz's imagined role came from a dream that his son had of his father visiting him (the son was one of the victims of the contagious disease), and that rumor, hysteria, and the prevalence of fanatical belief in vampires in the area did the rest (Riccardo 1993; Nickell 1995, 236).

Vampire Study

Given the many varieties of so-called vampires, there similarly exists a variety of vampirologists (those who study vampires). The earliest, of course, were the clerical vampire hunters, since vampirology is a branch of demonology (Stevenson 2002, 28–29). Bram Stoker (1897) created the quintessential fictional vampirologist in the form of Dr. Abraham Van Helsing, a Dutch medical specialist in rare diseases who abandoned rationalistic medicine and carried a superstitious bag of tricks containing a crucifix, wooden stake, and garlic.

Among today's vampirologists of sorts are the occultist (who treats vampires as real entities, as did Montague Summers [1880–1948] in his *The Vampire, His Kith and Kin* [1928] and *The Vampire in Europe* [1929]); the fictionalist (like Colin Wilson with his 1976 science-fiction novel *Space Vampires*, or Anne Rice, whose erotic horror series includes the 1976 *Interview with the Vampire* and the bestselling 1985 *The Vampire Lestat*); and the fantasizer (including those who merely role-play, those who adopt imaginative "vampire" lifestyles, and those who engage in blood fetishism for sexual or other purposes), among other "vampire" enthusiasts (Bunson 2000, 249; Ramsland 2002, 181; Dickinson 1997, Stevenson 2002, 149–58).

However, if we are to seriously add the root *–ology* to *vampire*, the presumably scholarly field thus described must represent more than credulity and fantasy. There is a serious field of study—embracing folklore, psychology, cultural anthropology, literature, history, and so on—that attempts to research and make sense of the various aspects of the vampire myth. To that study the term *vampirology* may well be applied.

Vampire Kits

One application of vampirology is the study of so-called "Vampire Killing Kits." I have been intrigued by these ever since I began to see them in Ripley's Believe It or Not! museums and elsewhere. But I chose the "or Not!": I was suspicious of them almost from the beginning.

I encountered one such item (labeled "Genuine Vampire Killing Kit c. 1850") in mid-2002 at Ripley's in Hollywood (see figure 11.1). It appears to be the same one referred to in a *Ripley's Believe It or Not! Encyclopedia of the Bizarre* (Mooney et al. 2002, 247), which states:

Figure 11.1. Reputed "Vampire Killing Kit" dates from circa 1850
(photograph by the author).

The handsome wooden box, lined with red velvet, contains everything a mortal might need to ward off an attack on the undead: a vial of holy water, a necklace of garlic, and a polished wooden stake for skewering the bloodsucker through the heart. But most effective of all: a small pistol in the shape of a crucifix, designed to shoot—you guessed it—silver bullets!

Another kit is found in the Ripley's museum in Niagara Falls, Ontario. It is dated "circa 1840's" and identified as "Made in Boston, USA," ostensibly for American travelers to Transylvania. If that seems an unusually small market for such a commercial item, consider this printed label in the lid, headed "Vampire Killing Kit":

This kit contains the items considered necessary for the protection of persons who travel into certain little known countries of Eastern Europe, where the populace are plagued with a particular manifestation of evil known as *Vampires*. Professor Ernst Blomberg respectfully requests that the purchaser of this kit, carefully studies his book in order, should evil manifestations become apparent, he is equipped to deal with them efficiently. Professor Blomberg wishes to announce his grateful thanks to that well known gunmaker of Liege, Nicholas Plomdeur whose help in the compiling of the special items, the silver bullets, &c, has been most efficient.

The items enclosed are as follows:

(1) An efficient pistol with its usual accouterments.
(2) Silver Bullets.
(3) An ivory crucifix.
(4) Powdered flowers of garlic.
(5) A wooden stake.
(6) Professor Blomberg's new serum.

Unfortunately, several other kits with similarly worded labels exist, yet, suspiciously, no two are alike. Many look like the result of old boxes and chests possibly having had their insides repartitioned and re-covered in velvet, then having been outfitted with a mishmash of ye olde items culled from antique shops. One such kit sold at Sotheby's on October 30, 2003, for a reported twelve thousand dollars and was accompanied by a "catalogue note": "Some vampire experts claim kits such as the present lot were very common in the eighteenth and nineteenth centuries among travelers to Eastern Europe. . . . Others claim that the kits originated in twentieth century America and are nothing more than romantic curiosities."

In fact, a bibliographic search conducted for me by Center for Inquiry Libraries director Timothy Binga failed to show any vampire book by a "Professor Ernst Blomberg." This is notwithstanding a pamphlet of dubious typography and plagiarized text ("Regarding" 2008).

One "Blomberg" kit was owned by the Henry J. Mercer Tool Museum in Doylestown, Pennsylvania, but officials became suspicious and had it tested. The labels' paper contained "fluorescent optical brightening agents" that date from after World War II. The glass in the magnifier also proved modern, and there were other signs of fakery, including the fact that the "silver" bullets were actually of pewter. (Indeed, the notion that silver bullets kill vampires is one largely redirected from werewolf legend by fiction and films [Bunson 2000, 240]).

The Blomberg kits appear universally to be fake. According to one research report ("Regarding" 2008), a man named Michael de Winter of Torquay, United Kingdom, admitted in December 2004 that "The whole VAMPIRE KILLING KIT myth is purely the result of my very fertile imagination and I produced 'The Original' in 1972." He wrote that he had hatched the scheme in order to sell a vintage, but substandard, pistol.

I purchased a different vampire kit—an assemblage of ludicrous items (including a test tube and dental mirror)—that I bought at a reasonable price for my collection (see figure 11.1). The seller stated that he had bought four kits over a seven-year period from a new-ager known as Sister Sarrie. She reportedly admits that they are "restored" but, the seller stated, "I also believe she embellishes them." He added, "Sister Sarrie says she's sold a lot of Spiritualist and Vampire kits over the years to theaters, sideshows and circuses" (Van Pelt 2003).

Do real antique vampire-killing kits exist? There may be a few apparently vintage kits, but, again, they may merely be old fakes. There appears to be no credible evidence for the marketing of such kits until after publication of Stoker's *Dracula* in 1897. In the novel, Van Helsing had a long leather bag that held a lantern, two wax candles, a matchbox, a soldering iron and plumbing solder (for sealing up leaden coffins), an oil lamp, a heavy hammer, a round wooden stake (to be driven through the vampire's heart), "operating knives" (for severing the head), garlic (for placing in the corpse's mouth), and a missal (or prayer book). On other occasions the doctor's small black medical bag contained items for protection from vampires (Stoker 1897, 268–69, 285–97).

It seems that Van Helsing's vampire kit is as authentic as they get, but, of course, it exists only in fiction. So does Dracula, and so do all vampires, many would insist, agreeing with Sherlock Holmes (in "The Adventure of the Sussex Vampire"): "Rubbish, Watson, rubbish! What have we to do with walking corpses who can only be held in their grave by stakes driven through their hearts? It's pure lunacy." But there *are* vampirologists; they are as real as—well, as real as I.

References

Bunson, Matthew. 2000. *The Vampire Encyclopedia*. New York: Grammercy Books.
Cruz, Joan Carroll. 1977. *The Incorruptibles*. Rockford, IL: Tan Books.
Dickinson, Joy. 1997. *Haunted City: An Unauthorized Guide to the Magical, Magnificent New Orleans of Anne Rice*. Secaucus, NJ: Citadel Press.
Leach, Maria, ed. 1984. *Funk & Wagnalls Standard Dictionary of Folklore, Mythology, and Legend*. New York: Harper & Row.
Marigny, Jean. 1994. *Vampires: Restless Creature of the Night*. New York: Harry N. Abrams.
Mooney, Julie, et al. 2002. *Ripley's Believe It or Not! Encyclopedia of the Bizarre*. New York: Black Dog & Leventhal.
Nickell, Joe. 1995. *Entities: Angels, Spirits, Demons, and Other Alien Beings*. Amherst, NY: Prometheus Books.

———. 2001. *Real-Life X-Files: Investigating the Paranormal.* Lexington, KY: University Press of Kentucky.

Polidoro, Massimo. 2006. "In Search of Dracula." *Skeptical Inquirer* 30, no. 2 (March/April): 25–27.

Rachleff, Owen S. 1971. *The Occult Conceit.* Chicago, IL: Cowles.

"Regarding Professor Blomberg." 2008. http://www.geocities.com/spookyland/ blomberg.html?20087 (accessed November 7, 2008).

Riccardo, Martin V. 1993. "Vampires—An Unearthly Reality." *Fate* (February): 63.

Robbins, Rossell Hope. 1959. *The Encyclopedia of Witchcraft and Demonology.* New York: Bonanza Books.

Stevenson, Jay. 2002. *The Complete Idiot's Guide to Vampires.* Indianapolis, IN: Alpha Books.

Stoker, Bram. 1897. *Dracula.* Reprint; New York: Barnes & Noble, 2003.

Summers, Montague. 1928. *The Vampire, His Kith and Kin*; reprinted New Hyde Park, NY: University Books, 1960.

———. 1929. *The Vampire in Europe.* London: Routledge & Kegan Paul.

Van Pelt, Tom. 2003. Letter to Rob McElroy. October 29.

Wilson, Colin, and Damon Wilson. 1992. *Unsolved Mysteries: Past and Present.* Chicago, IL: Contemporary Books.

Chapter 12

Searching for Vampire Graves

Given the ubiquitousness of vampires, those undead beings who are driven by bloodlust (and who thrive in movies like 2008's popular *Twilight*), it should not be surprising that historically there have been instances of reputed vampirism in the United States, notably in New England. And today there is a veritable vampire industry in New Orleans. I have investigated these cultural trends on site, tracking the legendary creatures to their very graves.

New England

New England has always been a mixture of both austere skepticism and passionate superstition. Vampire legends lurk in the latter. According to one vampirologist, "The presence in New England of a strongly rooted vampire mythology is something of an enigma to folklorists. There is quite simply no other area in all of North America with such a wealth of vampire lore" (Rondina 2008, 165).

One of the best-known examples is the case of nineteen-year-old Mercy Lena Brown in Exeter, Rhode Island, in 1892—a case that supposedly influenced Bram Stoker, author of *Dracula* (1897). As Katherine Ramsland concisely tells the story:

131

George Brown lost his wife and then his eldest daughter. One of his sons, Edwin, returned and once again became ill, so George exhumed the bodies of his wife and daughters. The wife and first daughter had decomposed, but Mercy's body—buried for three months—was fresh and turned sideways in the coffin, and blood dripped from her mouth. They cut out her heart, burned it, and dissolved the ashes in a medicine for Edwin to drink. However, he also died, and Mercy Brown became known as Exeter's vampire. (2002, 18)

Accounts of the exhumation in the *Providence Journal* of March 19 and 21, 1892, acknowledge that the Browns died of consumption (tuberculosis). They do not mention the corpse of Lena (as she was actually known) being turned on its side or blood dripping from the mouth. The exhumation was conducted by a young Harold Metcalf, MD, from the city of Wickford. "Dr. Metcalf reports the body in a state of natural decomposition, with nothing exceptional existing," stated the *Journal*. "When the doctor removed the heart and the liver from the body a quantity of blood dripped therefrom, but this he said was just what might be expected from a similar examination of almost any person after the same length of time from disease." The article added, "The heart and liver were cremated by the attendants" ("Exhumed" 1892).

A follow-up article ("Vampire" 1892) noted that the heart's blood was "clotted and decomposed . . . just what might be expected at that stage of decomposition." The correspondent acknowledged the custom of an afflicted person consuming the ashes to effect a cure, stating, "In this case the doctor does not know if this latter remedy was resorted to or not, and he only knows from hearsay how ill the son Edwin is, never having been called to attend him."

And so ends "Unarguably the best known incident of historical vampirism in America," indeed the story of "The Last Vampire" (Rondina 2008, 83, 99). However, there are many other reported cases typically involving consumption. The victim's lethargy, pale appearance, coughing of blood, and contagiousness all suggested to the superstitious the result of a "vampire's parasitic kiss" (Citro 1994, 71).

The Demon Vampire

In 2008 I went in search of vampire cases in Vermont. Apparently the earliest reported vampire incident took place in Manchester in 1793. Four years earlier, Captain Isaac Burton—a deacon in the congregational church—wed Rachel Harris. Judge John S. Pettibone (1786–1872) picks up the story:

> She was, to use the words of one who was well acquainted with her, "a fine, healthy, beautiful girl." Not long after they were married she went into a decline and after a year or so she died of consumption. Capt. Burton after a year or more married Hulda Powel, daughter of Esquire Powel by his first wife. Hulda was a very healthy, good-looking girl, not as handsome as his first wife. She became ill soon after they were married and when she was in the last stages of consumption, a strange infatuation took possession of the minds of the connections and friends of the family. They were induced to believe that if the vitals of the first wife could be consumed by being burned in a charcoal fire it would effect a cure of the sick second wife. Such was the strange delusion that they disinterred the first wife who had been buried about three years. They took out the liver, heart, and lungs, what remained of them, and burned them to ashes on the blacksmith's forge of Jacob Mead. Timothy Mead officiated at the altar in the sacrifice to the Demon Vampire who it was believed was still sucking the blood of the then living wife of Captain Burton. It was the month of February and good sleighing. Such was the excitement that from five hundred to one thousand people were present. This account was furnished me by an eye witness of the transaction.

Not only is Judge Pettibone's informant unnamed, but his manuscript (which still exists in the Manchester Historical Society [Harwood 2008]) is of uncertain date, although penned sometime between 1857 and 1872 (*Proceedings* 1930, 147). I located a Burton family history (Holman 1926) that makes no mention of the vampire tale but does confirm the sequence of marriages and deaths. (Captain Burton married Rachel Harris on March 8, 1789, and she died on February 1, 1790. He married Hulda Powell on January 4, 1791, and she succumbed on September 6, 1793.)

Therefore, the Pettibone account could be true. The salient point, however, is that belief in "the Demon Vampire" was indeed nothing more than a "strange delusion." Pettibone places the bizarre sacrifice about three years after Rachel's burial, which means the event occurred in early 1793, and Huldah died later that year. Clearly, anti-vampire magic was no cure for consumption.

I attempted to locate Rachel's grave. Isaac Burton (see figure 12.1) and his fourth wife, Dency Raymond (1774–1864), are buried together in the old section of Dellwood Cemetery in Manchester (Holman 1926, 25–28). The graves were relocated there from the old burial ground on the village green, today's courthouse site, where many old, unmarked graves are

Figure 12.1.
Deacon Isaac Burton's tombstone
is in Dellwood Cemetery,
Manchester, Vermont
(photograph by the author).

thought yet to remain (Harwood 2008). Among them may be the lost grave of the beautiful but unfortunate Rachel Harris.

On Woodstock Green

Another story comes from Woodstock, where sources claim a vampire's heart was burned on the public green around 1829 (see figure 12.2). The earliest account appeared in *The Journal of American Folklore* (Curtin 1889, 58–59). The story was later retold in the *Boston Transcript*, followed by an expanded version "Vampirism in Woodstock" in the October 9, 1890, issue of the *Vermont Standard* (quoted in Stephens 1970, 71–74). This gave the man's family name as Corwin. (Composite, garbled versions have since appeared [e.g., "Vampire Incidents" 2008].) According to the original source (Curtin 1889, 58):

> The man had died of consumption six months before and his body buried in the ground. A brother of the deceased fell ill soon after, and in a short time it appeared that he too had consumption; when this became known the family determined at once to disinter the body of the dead man and examine his heart. Then they reinterred the body, took the heart to the middle of Woodstock Green, where they

kindled a fire under an iron pot, in which they placed the heart, and burned it to ashes.

Unfortunately, not only was the story sixty years old at the time it appeared, but the writer failed to give any source other than an "old lady" in Woodstock who "said she saw the disinterment and the burning with her own eyes." The editor of the *Vermont Standard* added much supplementary material, claiming that the pot of ashes was buried under a seven-ton granite slab and that persons digging at the site a decade later encountered a sulfurous smell and smoke. This reference to the fires of Hell reveal the editor's writing as tongue-in-cheek, even sarcastic, and discredits his other details: the man's name as Corwin and burial in the Cushing Cemetery. Small wonder that no one of that name is buried in that graveyard—as shown by cemetery records (Stillwell and Proctor 1977) and confirmed by a search among the old tombstones (figure 12.3) by my wife and me (see also Crosier 1986; Wendlong 1990).

Misunderstanding the editor's satire, popular writers have tended either to give too much credence to the story or to debunk or dismiss it altogether. Possibly the original account did contain a nucleus of truth, an early account of consumption and superstitious belief associated with it.

Figure 12.2.
At Woodstock Green,
a vampire's heart was allegedly
burned and buried, circa 1829
(photograph by the author).

Figure 12.3.
The author looks for a vampire grave
at Cushing Cemetery,
Woodstock, Vermont
(author's photograph by Diana Harris).

The Killing Vine

Yet another old case, again involving consumption and associated superstition, has been reinterpreted by moderns as a "vampire incident" ("Vampire" 2008; Rondina 2008, 104). The story, in David L. Mansfield's *The History of the Town of Dummerston* (1884)—itself an account written some ninety years after the events and based on oral tradition—has become somewhat garbled by writers copying writers. Therefore, I tracked down a copy of the original text for study. It relates that Lieutenant Leonard Spaulding died of consumption in 1788, aged fifty-nine, father of eleven children. Mansfield states (1884, 27):

Although the children of Lt. Spaulding, especially the sons, became large, muscular persons, all but one or two died under 40 years of age of consumption, and their sickness was brief.

It is related by those who remember the circumstance; after six or seven of the family had died of consumption, another daughter was taken, it was supposed, with the same disease. It was thought she would die, and much was said in regard to so many of the family's dying of consumption when they all seemed to have the appearance of good health and long life. Among the superstitions of those days, we find it

Figure 12.4.
The Spaulding
Graves of
vampiric
legend lie in
Vermont's
Dummerston
Center
Cemetery
(photograph
by the
author).

Figure 12.5. The author uses chalk to enhance the slate tombstone of
Josiah Spaulding, topped with the familiar image of the angel of death
(author's photograph by Diana Harris).

was said that a vine or root of some kind grew from coffin to coffin, of those of one family, who died of consumption, and were buried side by side; and when the growing vine had reached the coffin of the last one buried, another one of the family would die; the only way to destroy the influence or effect, was to break the vine; take up the body of the last one buried and burn the vitals, which would be an effectual remedy: Accordingly, the body of the last one buried was dug up and the vitals taken out and burned, and the daughter, it is affirmed, got well and lived many years. The act, doubtless, raised her mind from a state of despondency to hopefullness [sic].

Now, Spaulding and his wife, Margaret (who died in 1827), were buried in separate cemeteries and in unmarked graves. However, I located all but two of the children's graves, including a row of six in the Dummerston Center Cemetery (see figures 12.4 and 12.5).

Unfortunately for the quaint legend related by oral tradition, the graves (whether or not linked by hidden underground vines) are not placed consecutively in the order of the family members' deaths. Neither did the last of the six, Josiah, die very close in time to the previous sibling's demise, since more than five and a half years passed since the death of John. Of course, the family may well have been plagued by consumption, and it is possible Josiah's body was disinterred and the vitals burned. In any event, he was indeed followed in death by one of Leonard Spaulding's daughters, as the legend states, since after he died only Olive remained alive. Apparently, she lived on for years, moving with a second husband to Brattleboro (Mansfield 1884, 26)—perhaps this being the secret of her having avoided the contagion!

In New Orleans

In sharp contrast to vampire legends of New England are those of New Orleans. While Louisiana indeed has a folk tradition of werewolves (the loup-garous of the Cajuns), the vampire culture there is not folklore but fakelore.

When I investigated various topics in the New Orleans area in 2000 (Nickell 2004, 140–61, 165–75), I found frequent references to vampires. The several nighttime tours focusing on cemeteries, voodoo, and ghosts invariably touted vampires as well, and guides (like mine) regaled tourists with spine-tingling tales of the "undead."

Anne Rice (born Howard Allen O'Brien in 1941) inspired legions of fans with her series of erotic horror novels, beginning with *Interview with the Vampire* (1976). Until she repudiated the genre, returned to her Catholic faith, and moved from New Orleans in 2005, many Rice devotees made pilgrimages to the Big Easy. Some walking tours included Rice's home or the location of the filming of *Interview*. There was even a tour book, *Haunted City: An Unauthorized Guide to the Magical, Magnificent New Orleans of Anne Rice* (Dickinson 1997).

According to Victor C. Klein, who has compiled two books of New Orleans ghost legends, "Throughout my extensive researches I have never encountered any tangible trace of Vampirism in Louisiana or New Orleans." He adds, "The genesis for such beliefs is directly attributable to the commercial imagination of Ms. Rice and the cerebrotonic endomorphs who, in their mad dash to establish a subjective species of identity and immortality, elevate her works to gospel status" (1999, 106). He also speaks of "the hyperbolic balderdash which spews forth from the black garbed tour guides who are more interested in money and sensationalism than accurate historical research" (1999, 64).

I recall one of the more responsible guides laughingly telling me how a customer once inquired about a particular grave featured in a Rice story and would not be convinced that the site was purely fictional. But I think the evidence shows that that grave is just as authentically vampiric as any real graves in New Orleans, New England, Europe, or elsewhere.

References

Bell, Michael E. 2008. "Vampire Incidents in New England." http://www.foodfor thedead.com/map.swf (accessed May 9, 2008).

Bunson, Matthew. 2000. *The Vampire Encyclopedia*. New York: Gramercy Books.

Citro, Joseph A. 1994. *Green Mountain Ghosts, Ghouls, and Unsolved Mysteries*. Boston, MA: Houghton Mifflin.

Crosier, Barney. 1986. "Vermont's Vampire Heart." *Rutland Herald*, October 26.

Curtin, Jeremiah. 1889. "European Folklore in the United States." *Journal of American Folklore* 2, no. 4 (March): 56–59.

Dickinson, Joy. 1997. *Haunted City: An Unauthorized Guide to the Magical, Magnificent New Orleans of Anne Rice*. Secaucus, NJ: Citadel Press.

"Exhumed the Bodies. . . ." 1892. *Provincetown Journal*, March 19. Reprinted in Rondina 2008, pp. 86–87 (below).

Hard, Walter R., Jr., and Janet C. Greene, eds. 1970. *Mischief in the Mountains*. Montpelier, VT: Vermont Life Magazine.

Harwood, Judy. 2008. Personal communication with the author, May 21 and July 9.

Holman, Winifred Lovering. 1926. *Descendants of Josiah Burton of Manchester, Vermont.* Concord, NH: Rumford Press.

Klein, Victor C. 1999. *New Orleans Ghosts II.* Metairie, LA: Lycanthrope Press.

Mansfield, David L. 1884. *The History of the Town of Dummerston.* Ludlow, VT: A. M. Hemenway.

Nickell, Joe. 2004. *The Mystery Chronicles: More Real-Life X-Files.* Lexington, KY: University Press of Kentucky.

Pettibone, Judge John S. N.d. "The Early History of Manchester." In *Proceedings* 1930, pp. 147–66 (below).

Proceedings of the Vermont Historical Society. 1930. New series 1, no. 4.

Ramsland, Katherine. 2002. *The Science of Vampires.* New York: Berkley Boulevard Books.

Rice, Anne. 1976. *Interview with the Vampire.* New York: Alfred A. Knopf.

Rondina, Christopher. 2008. *Vampires of New England.* Cape Cod, MA: On the Cape Publications.

Stevens, Rockwell. 1970. "The Vampire's Heart." In *Mischief in the Mountains*, edited by Walter Hard Jr. and Janet Greene, 71–81. Montpelier, VT: Vermont Life Magazine.

Stoker, Bram. 1897. *Dracula.* Reprinted; New York: Barnes & Noble, 2003.

Stillwell, Dorothy, and Dorothy L. Proctor. 1977. Cushing cemetery file, typescript at Norman Williams Public Library, Woodstock, VT.

"The Vampire Theory." 1892. *Providence Journal*, March 21. Reprinted in Rondina 2008, pp. 89–96 (above).

"Vampirism in Woodstock." 1890. *Vermont Standard*, October 9. Reprinted in Stevens 1970, pp. 71–74 (above).

Wendling, Kathy. 1990. "Woodstock's Vampire: The Heart of the Legend." *Vermont Standard*, October 25.

Chapter 13

Chupacabras!

I mitating the "cattle mutilation" hype of two decades before, during the 1990s reports of a bloodthirsty creature—*El Chupacabra* or "the goat-sucker"—began to spread throughout the Spanish-speaking areas of North and South America.

From Puerto Rico to Mexico

According to the Cox News Service (April 1996), "The creature suppos-edly is part space alien, part vampire and part reptile, with long sharp claws, bulging eyes and a Dracula-like taste for sucking blood from neck bites." In Puerto Rico, where the myth originated in 1995, "the creature has spawned something near hysteria" (see figure 13.1).

It reportedly attacked turkeys, goats, rabbits, dogs, cats, cows, and horses, sucking the blood from them. However, as Reuters reported, the Puerto Rico Agriculture Department dispatched a veterinarian to investigate. Officials then announced that all the animals had died under normal circumstances and that, contrary to claims, not one had been bled dry (Nickell 1996).

When the scare spread to Mexico in April of 1996, a scientific team staked out farmyards where the goatsucker had reportedly struck. Wild dogs were caught each time. A police official remarked, "I don't know about the rest of Mexico or the rest of the world, but here the goatsuckers are just dogs." He added: "There is just this huge psychosis. You see it

141

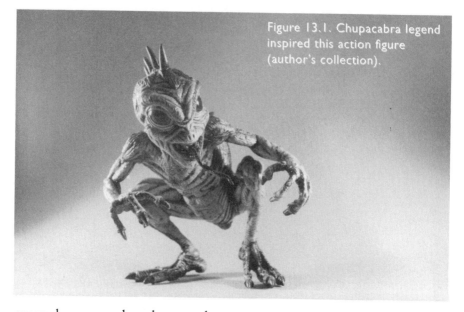

Figure 13.1. Chupacabra legend inspired this action figure (author's collection).

everywhere, even though everywhere we go we prove that there aren't any extraterrestrials or vampires" (Nickell 1996).

As media queries flooded into *Skeptical Inquirer*, I monitored the reports and developments and contacted our colleagues in Mexico City, Patricia and Mario Mendez-Acosta. They interviewed several veterinary pathologists who had conducted numerous necropsies on alleged victims of the goatsucker. Again, in every instance blood was still present in the dead animal. However, due to gravity causing the blood to settle (i.e., to drain downward), this can appear otherwise to laypersons.

Some news sources reported that a nurse who lived in a village near Mexico City had been attacked by the goatsucker. Actually, she simply fell and broke her arm, but her cries for help were misinterpreted by her grandmother. Neighbors rushing to her aid saw a black winged form; in reality, it was a flock of swallows, but thus the rumor was born. In another Mexican incident, a man who claimed he had been attacked by the goatsucker later confessed that it was a cover story for his having participated in a brawl (*Los Angeles Times*, May 19, 1996).

To the United States

By 1996, the myth had also reached Florida—as elsewhere, being initially spread by the Spanish-speaking media. The further migration came as no

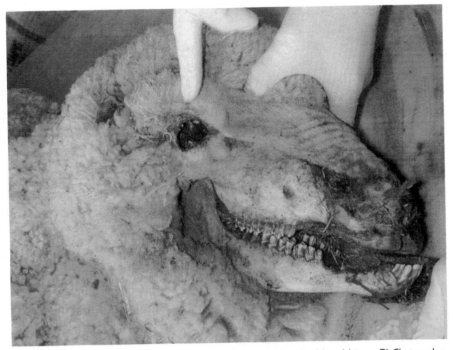

Figure 13.2. An Argentine ram was mutilated not by the bloodthirsty *El Chupacabra* but by predators (photograph used by permission of journalist Gabriel Alcalde).

surprise. Involving major livestock areas, the reported mutilations sparked conspiracy theories by UFOlogists, journalists, and local workers.

In the United States, "chupamania" found a ready breeding ground. Animal mutilation claims had been rife in the 1970s, although they were carefully investigated and attributed to the work of predators and scavengers (Frazier 1980; Nickell 1995, 115).

From initial media reports the craze quickly spread via electronic telecommunications. It became the first such monster craze to be diffused by the Internet. According to one media observer, it once took centuries for a monster legend to filter down through generations; now the process is similar except for the increased speed of dissemination (Trull n.d.). Soon the stories were featured in magazine articles, segments of books, and more. As early as 1997, a Hispanic-American cryptozoologist, Scott Corrales, had produced a book, *Chupacabras and Other Mysteries*. (In time, the creature—or at least an action-figure representation [see figure 13.1]— even graced the cover of my *The Mystery Chronicles: More Real-Life X-*

Files [Nickell 2004], although my discussion was investigatory rather than mystery-mongering or fantastic.)

During March 1996 the television talk show *Christina* (sort of a Spanish-language *Oprah*) did a segment on the Chupacabra panic. The Web site of Art Bell's sensationalistic radio show posted a photograph supposedly depicting a live Chupacabra, but instead showing a ridiculous entity that was, in fact, a museum statue (Coleman and Clark 1999, 62–63).

Soon, artistic renderings of the Chupacabra evolved into a vaguely humanesque entity—at least in walking upright on two legs and having "long, thin arms and hands with three long, skinny fingers with claws" (Coleman and Huyghe 1999, 80). Its large head, wraparound eyes and minimal other facial features (merely two nasal holes and a slash for a mouth) evoked the already popular concept of the gray alien of alleged extraterrestrial encounters (Coleman and Huyghe 1990, 80–81; Coleman and Clark 1999, 61–63).

Meanwhile, in Florida, prompted by local authorities and surrounded by members of the news media, a University of Miami veterinary professor, Alan Herron, performed a necropsy on a reputed Chupacabra victim. He cut open a dead goat to demonstrate that it had merely been bitten, not drained of its blood. Citing the bite wounds that were "suggestive of predation," Professot Herron concluded, "[a] pack of wild dogs did it."

"Of course," reported the Cox News Service, "that did little to calm the chupacabras frenzy" (Nickell 1996).

American Chupacabra lore took a new turn when three of the supposed monsters—or at least "three hairless doglike creatures"—became roadkill near Cuero, DeWitt County, Texas, in 2007. When a fourth was discovered in 2008, DNA tests showed the creature was *Canis latrans*, the common coyote. However, a second round of tests at the University of California, Davis—with special expertise in animal forensic science—revealed that it was a cross between a coyote and a Mexican wolf. As to the lack of hair, some speculated that it was due to a defective gene, but a pathologist at Texas Tech University attributed it to sarcoptic mange, caused by burrowing skin mites (Mitter 2008). Given a spate of other bizarre, hairless creatures (such as the "Chinese Yeti" mentioned in chapter 5), Loren Coleman has observed that many of these may be dogs or other animals suffering from mange.

Investigating in Argentina

Not surprisingly, the Chupacabra contagion also infected Latin America. As background, it is worth noting that the face of the Argentine *pampas* (plains) was altered in the sixteenth century by the arrival of feral livestock that displaced the native rhea (American ostrich) and guanaco (ancestor of the llama and alpaca). The Spaniards brought such domestic animals as horses, cattle, sheep, pigs, and poultry (Bernhardson 2004, 633).

Unsurprisingly, therefore, given normal predation on livestock, the animal-mutilation claims took hold in the region. Typical of the reports I collected was "Chupacabras Attack Ranches in Argentina" (Trainor 2000).

In 2005, while visiting Argentina for the First Latin American Conference on Critical Thinking in Buenos Aires, I was able to spend a day at a horse ranch in the pampas north of the city. In addition to having an open-pit barbecue lunch, going horseback riding, and experiencing other entertainments, I was able to talk with the head gaucho who told me (with my guide translating) that the Chupacabra claims were nonsense and that there were certainly no such mutilations of horses at this ranch or any credible attacks on cattle or other livestock nearby (Romero 2005). One of the five brothers who own the ranch was similarly dismissive of the idea that Chupacabras were on the loose (Rossiter 2005).

At the conference, I met journalist Gabriel Alcalde of Santa Rosa who generously shared his knowledge of the local phenomenon. He related that almost one hundred cases of animal mutilation were reported in La Pampa and Buenos Aires Provinces between May and August 2002 (see figure 13.2). However, he noted that research conducted by the National Service for Food and Agriculture (SENASA), with the Veterinary College of National University of the Center of the Province of Buenos Aires (as well as other universities in the area where mutilated livestock were discovered), had found mundane explanations. In a report, SENASA concluded:

> The deaths can be attributed to natural causes. Under direct and close observation it could be ascertained that the injuries to the tissues and organs were caused by predators. Histological studies done on the carcasses showed conclusively that no special tools had been used to produce the cuts, e.g., cauterizing scalpels.

The conclusion was that the animals' deaths were due to such natural causes as alimentary deficiencies, and that the mutilations were subsequently caused by predators, including field mice. The report stated that "in all the cases under review there were traces of bird, carrion (fox), and rodent (mice) feces on the carcasses and near the dead animals."

And so the Chupacabras were vanquished, although Gabriel Alcade pointed out that many Argentines denied the scientific evidence and "continued to believe the spellbinding stories concocted by the media." He told me that he felt the real mutilation was that which had been done to critical thinking.

References

Alcalde, Gabriel. 2005. Personal communication with the author. October 20.

Bernhardson, Wayne. 2004. *Moon Handbooks Argentina*. Emeryville, CA: Avalon Travel Publishing.

Coleman, Loren, and Jerome Clark. 1999. *Cryptozoology A to Z*. New York: Fireside.

Corrales, Scott. 1997. *Chupacabras and Other Mysteries*. Murfreesboro, TN: Greenleaf.

Frazier, Kendrick. 1980. "Cattle Mutilations: Mystery Deflated, Mutologists Miffed." *Skeptical Inquirer 5*, no. 1 (Fall): 2–6.

Los Angeles Times. 1996. May 19.

Nickell, Joe. 1995. *Entities*. Amherst, NY: Prometheus Books.

———. 1996. "Goatsucker Hysteria." *Skeptical Inquirer* 20, no. 5 (September/October): 12.

———. 2004. *The Mystery Chronicles*. Lexington, KY: University Press of Kentucky, pp. 28–30.

Romero, Luis. 2005. Interview by the author with guide Paola Luski translating. September 16.

Rossiter, Patricio. 2005. Interview by the author with guide Paola Luski translating. September 16.

Trainor, Joseph. 2000. "Chupacabras Attack Ranches in Argentina." *UFO Roundup 5*, no. 28 (July 13). http://bbs.destinationspace.net/view.php3?bn=dspace_ufoenigma&key=963669845&first=9 (accessed September 9, 2005).

Trull, Donald. N.d. Cited in Coleman and Clark, 1999, p. 62 (above).

Chapter 14

Other Supernaturals

I n addition to werewolves, vampires, and Chupacabras, there are many other fanciful man-beasts that—so to speak—people the supernatural realm. These include Devil Men, the Zanzibar Demon, and Zombies— each treated in turn here.

Devil Men

In the belief of many fundamentalist Christians, Satan is not merely a personification of evil, but its very real embodiment. As such he is supposedly the power behind sorcerers (warlocks and witches). Frequently he is depicted as a serpent (signifying his lowly position and his cunning, poisonous ways) or, alternately, he is portrayed as a man-goat figure (apparently after pre-Christian deities like Pan, the goatlike god of fields and forests from Greek mythology). In this form he typically has whiskers, horns, cloven hooves, and a tail (Rachleff 1971, 107; Cavendish 1975, 170–71).

From time to time evidence is brought forth that supposedly confirms the existence of the goatlike satan. For example, there was the nineteenth-century case of "the Devil's hoofprints" in the county of Devon, England, that proved to be a contagious rash of misperceptions (Nickell 2001, 10–17). Then there was the "Jersey Devil," a phantom folklore creature with hooves, an animalian head, wings, and tail. It was given embodiment in a famous hoax of 1909 in which a caged kangaroo was outfitted with fake wings and prompted to leap at spectators by being prodded with a stick (Nickell 1995, 243–44).

Again, there were the cloven-hoofed tracks allegedly discovered outside the infamous "Amityville Horror" house in Long Island. Supposedly those of a demon, they were, however, part of another elaborate hoax (Nickell 2004, 73–77).

I had my own close encounter with a "devil" in 1971. It was in the form of a supposedly mummified little creature I came across in the window of a Toronto curio shop. It had budding horns, fangs, clawlike nails, a long tail, and realistic hooves: a devil-baby mummy! Apparently I showed too much curiosity (or skepticism) about the small creature, because the owner snapped at me that it was not for sale and that I should not interest myself in it. I did wrest from him the statement that he had bought it from an Irish museum twelve years before. Later the figure was moved to the rear of the store, but a photographer I commissioned obtained a photo during the shop's off hours by shooting through the window with a long-range lens (see figure 14.1).

Still later, I sent a friend to the store. Using a wad of cash to get the

Figure 14.1. A reputed devil baby mummy appeared for a time in a Toronto curio shop, 1971 (author's photograph).

proprietor's attention, my friend received an offer to buy the sinister creature for a five-figure sum. Before leaving, he was able to get a close look at
the curio, observing that the hair had been glued on.

Subsequently, in a book titled *Vampires, Zombies, and Monster Men*,
I discovered a photograph of a similar creature—or rather a pair of them,
their arms folded in the repose of death. Headed "Clahuchu and his
Bride," a sign affixed to the creatures' coffin claimed: "These shrunken
mummified figures were found in a crude tomblike cave on the island of
Haiti in 1740 by a party of French marines. They are supposed to be the
remains of a lost tribe of 'Ju-Ju' or Devil Men—who, after death followed
a custom of shrinking & mummifying their dead." The sign concluded:
"Are they real? We don't know, but . . . *X-Rays showed skin, horn, &
hooves human!*" There was, astonishingly, however, no mention of a
skeleton. Painted beneath the sign were these mumbo-jumbo words:
"YENOH M'I DLOC!" (Farson 1976, 32). My cryptanalytical (code-
solving) interests were piqued, and I soon discovered that reading each
word backward in turn yields the prankish message, "Honey I'm Cold!"—
presumably an indication of the seriousness with which we should
approach the "devil" figures (Nickell 1995, 111–15).

There are other such creatures. One had been in the possession of a cult
leader who claimed it was his satanic offspring, which was stillborn. As
described by John Anderson in his *Psychic Phenomena Unveiled: Confes-
sions of a New Age Warlock* (n.d., 103–104, 108), it had "the shape of a
small petrified body. The skin was very dark, almost black. Its feet were
those of a goat. The body appeared to be half human, half animal, the face
long, with a pointed chin." Later, Anderson heard from a former cult
member who had managed to sneak a closer look at the figure in the day-
light. He said: "Impressive all right. An impressive papier-mâché and
plaster of paris job . . . not the remains of some mutant offspring of Satan."

Figures like this are reminiscent of those seen in many carnival
sideshows. A showman named William Nelson, who once managed the
show wagon of the Pawnee Bill Wild West Show, began to sell "mummified curiosities" in 1909. These included a "Devil Child" that sold for
"$15 cash" or, "with 8 × 10 [sideshow] banner, $35.00"

An elaborate figure of this genre is the modern "Devil Man," what is
known in carnival parlance as a *gaffed* (faked) oddity. The touring figure,
owned by carny authority James Taylor, is the creation of sideshow banner
painter and "gaff artist" Mark Frierson, who fashioned it from papier-
mâché, pieces of bone, and craft supplies (Nickell 2005, 338).

Zanzibar Demon

The scene is modern-day Zanzibar, where a terrible monster, the infamous "popobawa," is swooping into bedrooms at night and raping men—particularly skeptical men. The demonic beast's name comes from the Swahili words for *bat* and *wing*, and indeed the creature is described as having, in addition to a dwarf's body with a single cyclopean eye, small pointed ears, and batlike wings and talons. According to local villagers, it is especially prone to attack "anybody who doesn't believe" (McGreal 1995).

One 1995 victim was a quiet-spoken peasant, a farmer named Mjaka Hamad, who said he does not believe in spirits. He first thought he was having a dream. However, "I could feel it," he said, "something pressing on me. I couldn't imagine what sort of thing was happening to me. You feel as if you are screaming with no voice." He went on to say: "It was just like a dream but then I was thinking it was this popobawa and he had come to do something terrible to me, something sexual. It is worse than what he does to women."

The demon struck Zanzibar in 1970 and again briefly in the 1980s. According to the *Guardian*, "Even those who dismiss the attacks as superstition nonetheless admit that for true believers they are real. Zanzibar's main hospital has treated men with bruises, broken ribs and other injuries, which the victims blame on the creature" (McGreal 1995).

I was given an article on the Zanzibaran affair by a colleague who half-jokingly remarked, "Here's a case for you to solve." I read a few paragraphs and replied, "I have solved it."

I only needed to recall some of my earlier research to realize that the popobawa is essentially a Zanzibaran version of a physiological and psychological phenomenon known as a "waking dream." One of the characteristics of such a dream, known more technically as a *hypnopompic* or *hypnagogic* hallucination (depending on whether one is, respectively, waking up or going to sleep), is a feeling of being weighted down or even paralyzed. Alternately, one may "float" or have an out-of-body experience. Other characteristics include extreme vividness of the dream and bizarre and/or terrifying content (Baker and Nickell 1992, 226–27; Nickell 1995, 41, 46, 55, 59, 131, 157, 209, 214, 268, 278).

Similar feelings were also experienced by persons in the Middle Ages who reported nighttime visitations of an *incubus* (a male demon that lay with women) or a *succubus* (which took female form and lay with men). In Newfoundland the visitor was called the "Old Hag" (Ellis 1988). In the infamous West Pittston, Pennsylvania, "haunted house" case of 1986, tenant Jack Smurl claimed he was raped by a succubus. As "demonologist" Ed Warren described it:

> He was asleep in bed one night and he was awakened by this haglike woman who paralyzed him. He wanted to scream out, of course—he was horrified by what he saw, the woman had scales on her skin and white, scraggly hair, and some of her teeth were missing—but she paralyzed him in some manner. Then she mounted him and rode him to her sexual climax. (Warren and Warren 1989, 105–106)

Such accounts come from widespread places and times. For example, consider this interesting encounter, which occurred in the seventeenth century. It concerned one Anne Jeffries, a country girl from Cornwall. According to scholar Bill Ellis:

> In 1645 she apparently suffered a convulsion and was found, semi-conscious, lying on the floor. As she recovered, she began to recall in detail how she was accosted by a group of six little men. Paralyzed, she felt them swarm over her, kissing her, until she felt a sharp pricking sensation. Blinded, she found herself flying through the air to a palace filled with people. There, one of the men (now her size) seduced her, and suddenly an angry crowd burst in on them and she was again blinded and levitated. She then found herself lying on the floor surrounded by her friends. (1988, 264, 633)

This account obviously has striking similarities to many UFO abduction accounts—some of which, like those of Whitley Strieber's own "abduction" experiences described in *Communion* (1988), are fully consistent with hypnopompic or hypnagogic hallucinations (Baker and Nickell 1992). Still other entities that have appeared in classic waking dreams are ghosts and angelic visitors (Nickell 1995).

As these examples illustrate, although the popobawa seems at first a unique, Zanzibarian creature, it is actually only a variant of a well-known phenomenon—one that Western skeptics, at least, have little to fear.

Zombies

In popular culture, the zombie is a mindless, walking corpse. An element of the Haitian cult of vodun, or voodoo, *zonbi* is a word loaded with numerous meanings and implications. Technically, a zonbi is a portion of the human soul that is stolen and forced to work.

The common zombie is called *zonbi astral*, the spirit of a deceased person that is captured magically—by a *bokor* (or sorcerer)—and contained, typically, in a bottle. An empty rum bottle is often used, and after the spirit is captured in it, it is adorned with magical charms. The resulting fetish is thus alive with spirit and capable, voodoo practitioners believe, of working on behalf of the one who possesses it—effecting healings, removing bad spirits, and performing other magical duties. An excellent introduction to the subject is Elizabeth McAlister's "A Sorcerer's Bottle: The Visual Art of Magic in Haiti" (in Cosentino 1995, 305–21).

Another type of zonbi is the rare living-dead entity in the form of a reanimated corpse. According to an authoritative source (Leach 1984, 1195):

> The sorcerer digs up the body after its interment, using it as he wishes. It is believed that if the zombi is allowed to eat food flavored with salt, or, in some districts, if he is allowed to look on the sea, he will return to his grave. It is held that, if necessary, a zombi can be turned into an animal, slaughtered, and the meat sold in the market, whence derives the assertion often met with among Haitian peasants in documenting belief that they have not only seen zombies but have bought their flesh. This, it is thought, can be distinguished by the fact that such meat will spoil much more readily than ordinary meat.

Popularized by Hollywood, the legend of zombies was boosted by the 1932 movie *White Zombie*, starring Bela Lugosi. It has since rivaled in movie popularity the vampire, the undead mummy (played by Boris Karloff), and the Frankenstein monster. According to Colin Wilson and Damon Wilson, "No one who has seen a film like *King of the Zombies* can ever forget the shot of a zombie marching on like a robot while someone fires bullet after bullet into its chest" (1992, 413).

But what about stories telling of "real" zombies? They are difficult to investigate, not only because of their remoteness but also because many are anecdotal accounts on par with Elvis Presley sightings, angelic visitations, or extraterrestrial encounters. Some investigators suggest that persons targeted as enemies may be "zombified" by the use of some "quick-acting poison" (Wilson and Wilson 1992, 413–17). Owen S. Rachleff, in *The Occult Conceit* insists: "The cataleptic status achieved by some of the celebrants of voodoo sometimes becomes so severe as to be permanent" (1971, 218). Still another theory, advanced by the director of Port-au-Prince's Psychiatric Center, holds that so-called zombies have merely been drugged and so enslaved as agricultural workers (*Reader's* 1982, 113).

Wade Davis, an ethnobotanist, claimed in his 1985 book *Serpent and the Rainbow* that zombification could be caused by "zombie powder," which reportedly contained the poison tetrodotoxin (TTX). He presented the case of a man named Clairvius Narcisse who died and was buried on May 2, 1962. After eighteen years, however, a man claiming to be Narcisse surfaced—rather literally, he claimed. He convinced a relative and others that he had been drugged into a state of suspended animation and could remember being buried and subsequently disinterred by a bokor and his helpers. He was enslaved on a plantation for two years but escaped with other zombies in an uprising. He supposedly spent the following years wandering about, looking for his family.

It is quite a tale, but it must be said that no serious, scientific investigation was conducted. The grave of Clairvius Narcisse was not opened to see if his body was missing, and, of course, DNA testing had not yet come to the fore (Hahn 2007). Psychologist Terence Hines (2008), writing in *Skeptical Inquirer*, observes that TTX produces symptoms that are markedly different from those of alleged zombies. He suggests Davis's book "is an excellent example of a credulous foreigner taken advantage of by local tricksters and is full of scientific absurdities." Other alleged zombies have similarly been discredited.

African American writer Zora Neale Hurston in her book *Tell My Horse* (1937) related the case of a woman who appeared in ragged clothing in 1936, claiming to be a woman named Felicia Felix-Mentor who died in 1907. However, psychiatrist Louis P. Mars, reporting in the journal *Man: A Record of Anthropological Science* (1945), said of Hurston: "Evidently she got her information from the simple village folk, whose minds were conditioned to believing the real existence of a super-human phenomenon. Miss Hurston herself, unfortunately, did not go beyond the mass hysteria to verify her information, nor in any way attempt to make a scientific explanation of the case." Dr. Mars, noting that the real Felicia Felix-Mentor had been lame due to a broken left leg, x-rayed both of the claimant's legs and found no evidence of any fracture. He disagnosed the woman as schizophrenic.

At least two modern cases of alleged zombification were disproved by DNA testing. One claimant was diagnosed with brain damage resulting from anoxia; the other appeared to suffer from fetal alcohol syndrome (Hahn 2007).

As with reports of other strange creatures, however, it appears likely that not all accounts of zombies have a single, simple explanation. Least likely, of course, is the supernatural notion that zombies really are the "walking dead."

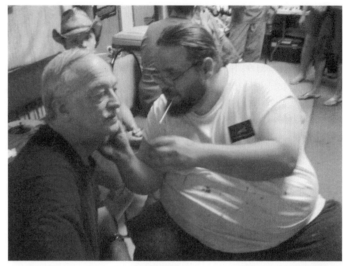

Figure 14.2.
Makeup artist
applies prosthetics
to author before
coloring and
blending
(author's
photograph).

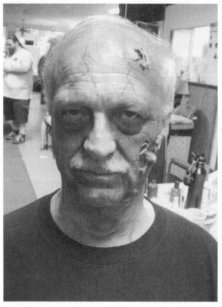

Figure 14.4 The author, drizzled with
"blood," appears on location for
The Final Night and Day
(author's photograph).

Figure 14.3. Transformation into
a zombie is almost complete
(author's photograph).

Nevertheless, on June 19, 2010, I became a zombie of the popular type—a "real" one, in the carnival/circus sideshow sense of that word: with real makeup, real fake blood, real phony trance state. This was for a new horror movie, *The Final Night and Day*, produced by DefTone Pictures Studios of Hamburg, New York, and slated for March 2011 release on DVD. Some 325 zombie extras and "hero" zombies (those with elaborate makeup due to their proximity to the camera), participated, and I was in the latter group. My makeup was done by Rod Durick of Zombified Studios of Lackawanna, New York, who did the silicone prosthetics, and his associate Tammy Janinum, who colored and blended it into a suitably ghoulish effect (see figures 14.2–14.4). Later on the set, I got liberal applications of "blood," and for the next few hours, from dusk to midnight, shuffled and lurched along the main street of "Metzburgh" (Angola, New York) in my zombie role: less a Haitian-voodoo style entity than a type of Hollywoodized ghoul that has taken on, so to speak, a life of its own. The irony is that it may be just as authentic as any other.

Zombie slaves embody the notion of induced mind/body control. The concept is pervasive, with paranormal entities typically having some means of monitoring mortals as a prelude to control. Examples range from mythological beings—like Cupid, whose magical arrows infected men's hearts with love, and Morpheus, who formed sleepers' dreams—to superstitious belief in angelic guidance, demonic possession, voodoo hexes, and the like. Folklore told of abductions to fairyland from which people returned with addled wits or sapped vitality. Popular literature brought such examples as Bram Stoker's *Dracula* (1897) and the mesmerizing Svengali in George du Maurier's *Trilby* (1894). Science fiction helped develop the alien-takeover concept with such movies as *The Invasion of the Body Snatchers* (1956). A 1967 *Star Trek* episode, "Errand of Mercy," featured a "mindsifter," a device used by the alien Klingons to probe prisoners' thoughts during interrogations (Okuda and Okuda 1997, 141, 303; Nickell 2001, 204–205).

References

Baker, Robert A., and Joe Nickell. 1992. *Missing Pieces: How to Investigate Ghosts, UFOs, Psychics, and Other Mysteries*. Amherst, NY: Prometheus Books.

Cavendish, Richard. 1975. *The Powers of Evil*. New York: Dorset Press.

Cosentino, Donald J., ed. 1995. The Sacred Arts of Haitian Vodou. Los Angeles, CA: UCLA Fowler Museum of Cultural History.

Ellis, Bill. 1988. "The Varieties of Alien Experience." *Skeptical Inquirer* 12, no. 3 (Spring): 263–69.

Farson, Daniel. 1976. *Vampires, Zombies, and Monster Men*. New York: Doubleday.

Hahn, Patrick D. 2007. "Dead Man Walking." Biology Online, September 4. http://www.biology-online.org/articles/dead_man_walking.html (accessed June 16, 2010).

Hines, Terence. 2008. "Zombies and Tetrodotoxin." *Skeptical Inquirer* 32, no. 3 (May/June): 60–62.

Leach, Maria, ed. 1984. *Funk & Wagnall's Standard Dictionary of Folklore, Mythology, and Legend*. New York: Harper & Row.

Mars, Louis P. 1945. "The Story of Zombi in Haiti." *Man: A Record of Anthropological Science* 45, no. 22 (March/April): 38–40.

McGreal, Chris. 1995. "Zanzibar Diary." *Guardian*, October 2.

Nickell, Joe. 1995. *Entities: Angels, Spirits, Demons, and Other Alien Beings*. Amherst, NY: Prometheus Books.

———. 2001. *Real-Life X-Files: Investigating the Paranormal*. Lexington, KY: University Press of Kentucky.

———. 2004. *The Mystery Chronicles: More Real-Life X-Files*. Lexington, KY: University Press of Kentucky.

———. 2005. *Secrets of the Sideshows*. Lexington, KY: University Press of Kentucky.

Okuda, Michael, and Denise Okuda. 1997. *The Star Trek Encyclopedia*. New York: Pocket.

Rachleff, Owen S. 1971. *The Occult Conceit*. Chicago, IL: Cowles.

Reader's Digest Mysteries of the Unexplained. 1982. Pleasantville, NY: Reader's Digest Association.

Streiber, Whitley. 1988. *Communion: A True Story*. New York: Avon.

Warren, Ed, and Lorraine Warren, with Robert David Chase. 1989. *Ghost Hunters*. New York: St. Martin's Paperbacks.

Wilson, Colin, and Damon Wilson. 1992. *Unsolved Mysteries: Past and Present*. Chicago, IL: Contemporary Books.

Part 4
Extraterrestrials

Chapter 15

Alien Monster at Flatwoods

The modern wave of UFOs was triggered on June 24, 1947, when businessman Kenneth Arnold, flying his private airplane over Washington state's Cascade Mountains, reported seeing some objects flying with a motion like "a saucer skipped across water." Thus the misnomer "flying saucers" was born. Arnold gave conflicting versions of what he saw, but it now seems likely that he was a victim of "mountain-top mirages." My colleague, USAF Major James McGaha (2006), a UFO expert, told me that the conditions under which Arnold saw the strange objects—clear skies, smooth air, a potential temperature inversion, and the angle of the sun from the horizon—were ideal for producing just such mirage effects.

Other UFO reports soon described encounters with their supposed alien astronauts. Among them was the case of the Flatwoods Monster, which was launched on September 12, 1952, and was never completely explained. I investigated this story in 2000.

The Incident

In modern police parlance, a long-unsolved homicide or other crime may be known as a "cold case," a term we might borrow for such paranormal mysteries as that of the Flatwoods Monster.

The story began about 7:15 p.m. At the little village of Flatwoods, in

159

Braxton County, West Virginia, some boys were playing on the school playground when, suddenly, they saw a fiery UFO streaking across the sky. It seemed to land on a hilltop nearby. Running to the nearby home of Mrs. Kathleen May, a local beautician, the youngsters obtained a flashlight and went up the hill to investigate. The group now included Mrs. May and her two sons, Eddie (thirteen years old) and Freddie (fourteen), along with Neil Nunley (fourteen), Gene Lemon (seventeen), and Tommy Hyer and Ronnie Shaver (both ten). They were accompanied by Lemon's dog.

What happened next is the subject of endless debate. Gray Barker, who wrote fanciful UFO tales for *Fate* magazine, interviewed members of the group later. Neil Nunley provided the least emotional account. He was in the lead as the group hastened to the hill's crest, spotting in the distance a pulsing red light.

Suddenly, Gene Lemon aimed his flashlight at a pair of shining eyes peering out of the darkness. There was a tall, "manlike" being with a round red "face" that was surrounded by a "pointed, hood-like shape." The creature's dark body was indistinct but would afterward be described by some as green with—Mrs. May would report—drapelike folds. After a moment the monster suddenly emitted a high-pitched hissing sound and swept, in a gliding fashion, toward the group. Terrified, Lemon screamed, dropped the flashlight, and fled, followed by the others.

They reported their encounter to a few locals and then to the sheriff and a deputy (after the officers returned from investigating a report of an airplane crash). The site was searched but nothing was seen or smelled— even though the eyewitnesses had reported a pungent mist, and that afterward some had become nauseated. The next day, a reporter from the *Braxton Democrat*, A. Lee Stewart Jr., discovered what he described as "skid marks" in the roadside field, together with an "odd gummy deposit"—assumed to be traces of the landed flying saucer (Barker 1953).

Barker's article (1953) and later book (1956) helped propel the Flatwoods Monster case into UFO history. Other reports followed, including those by paranormal mystery writer Ivan T. Sanderson (1952, 1967) and early UFOlogist Major Donald E. Kehoe. Some accounts are filled with garbled details, such as those by Peter Brookesmith (1995) and David Ritchie (1994). A generally sensible, factual version of events is Jerome Clark's *The UFO Encyclopedia* (1998), which terms the case "one of the most bizarre UFO encounters of all time."

Investigating at Flatwoods

In mid-2000, I investigated the long-cold case at Flatwoods (see figure 15.1), speaking with resident Johnny Lockard (ninety-five years old; see figure 15.2), who told me that the fiery object the boys had seen had been recognized by local residents as a meteor. Indeed, a former newspaper editor stated, "There is no doubt that a meteor of considerable proportion flashed across the heavens that Friday night since it was visible in at least three states—Maryland, Pennsylvania, and West Virginia" (Byrne 1966). Astronomers confirmed the identification (Kehoe 1953; Reese 1952). Air Force investigators determined that the meteor "merely appeared to be landing when it disappeared over the hill" (Keyhoe 1953). That illusion was also responsible for the mistaken report investigated by the sheriff of a plane that crashed in flames.

Other illusions came into play. The red, pulsating light the boys had seen as they approached the hilltop was probably only "the light from a nearby plane beacon," and Sanderson (1952) acknowledged that no fewer than three such beacons were "in sight all the time on the hilltop." (However, he, busily promoting a UFO mystery, dismissed this obvious explanation.) As to the landing traces, Johnny Lockard's son, Max, explained to me how *he* had caused them inadvertently: Responding to the reported incident that evening, he had driven his 1942 Chevy pickup up the roadway to see what he might discover. As a consequence, he left the skid marks while getting back onto the lane from the field, and the discovered gunk came from his leaking oil pan. In June 2000, he drove me in his modern pickup to retrace his actions in 1952 (figure 15.3).

Other elements in the Flatwoods incident have probable explanations as well. The nauseating odor was, conceded Sanderson (1967), "almost surely derived

Figure 15.1. Sign at Flatwoods, West Virginia, heralds "Home of the Green Monster" (photograph by the author).

from a kind of grass that abounds in the area." The actual nausea, the Air Force investigators reportedly concluded, "was a physical effect brought on by the fright" (Keyhoe 1953). But if all this is so, what then was the terrifying creature? Did it, too, have a terrestrial origin?

The Flatwoods Monster

Known as "the Phantom of Flatwoods," "the Braxton County Monster," "the Visitor from Outer Space," and other appellations (Byrne 1966), the Flatwoods Monster was unlikely to have been the effect of vapor from a falling meteor ("Monster" 1952) or Mrs. May's own eventual notion that it was "a secret plane the government was working on" (Marchal 1966). Freddie May did tell me that his mother no longer knew *what* she saw (2000).

I am in agreement with most previous investigators that the incident was not a hoax. I believe the witnesses did see and experience something that can be explained as a known West Virginia creature—even its apparent towering height. They described it as having a somewhat "man-like shape," with a "round," "fiery orange" face, surrounded by a "hood-like shape" and "shining," "animal eyes." It had "terrible claws" and moved with "a gliding motion as if afloat in mid air." Its cry was "something between a hiss and a high-pitched squeal" (Barker 1953, 1956; Sanderson 1967).

They described, in other words, a barn owl. That creature, *Tyto alba*, indeed has a roundish face appearing as if "shrouded in a closely fitting hood." It typically has a white facial disc and underparts, the female having "some darker buff or tawny color." Its eyes exhibit bright eyeshine, and it does indeed have sharp, curved talons that may be prominently extended. The barn owl's flight is often with "long glides," and when accidentally disturbed it makes an "erratic getaway" while making a "shrill rasping hiss" (Blanchan 1925; Peterson 1980; Cloudsley-Thompson et al. 1983; "Barn Owl" 2000; for a more detailed comparison and additional sources, see Nickell 2000).

Of course, the barn owl does not stand ten feet tall. However, we should note that, as Barker (1953) reported of the Flatwoods Monster, "descriptions from the waist down are vague; most of the seven said this part of the figure was not under view." These perceptions are consistent—see figure 15.4—with a large barn owl (the female is typically the larger of the species) perched on a tree limb. The locale where the Flatwoods Mon-

Figure 15.2.
Johnny Lockard, ninety-five,
recalls the monster incident
(photograph by the author).

ster was encountered—near a large oak on a partly wooded hilltop on the outskirts of town—tallies with the habitat of *Tyto alba* (Blanchan 1925; Peterson 1980).

It is unlikely that the seven impressionable witnesses had ever seen a barn owl under such frightening nighttime conditions. However, to adapt an old adage, if it looked like a barn owl, acted like a barn owl, and hissed, then likely it was a barn owl.

Despite the foregoing evidence, flying saucer die-hards and conspiracy theorists have latched onto the case, notably one Frank C. Feschino Jr., author of *The Braxton County Monster: The Cover-up of the Flatwoods Monster Revealed* (2004). Actually, it reveals no such thing but merely illustrates

Figure 15.3.
Flatwoods, West Virginia, resident
Max Lockard identifies site of
1952 "monster" sighting
(photograph by the author).

just how confused memories can become after half a century and how an amateur investigator can inflate a tale. Feschino does not even reference my investigative report from *Skeptical Inquirer* science magazine (Nickell 2000). He leaves that to the foreword written by UFO conspiracy promoter Stanton T. Friedman, whose previous lost causes include the "Roswell incident." Friedman was taken in by the amateurishly forged "MJ-12" documents in that case (Nickell with Fischer 1992, 81–105). *Caveat emptor*, "let the buyer beware."

References

Barker, Gray. 1953. "The Monster and the Saucer." *Fate* (January): 12–17.

———. 1956. *They Knew Too Much about Flying Saucers*. New York: Tower.

"Barn Owl." 2000. Auburn University College of Veterinary Medicine. http://www.vetmed.auburn.edu/.

Blanchan, Neltje. 1925. *Birds Worth Knowing*. Garden City, NY: Nelson Doubleday, pp. 180–82.

Brookesmith, Peter. 1995. *UFO: The Complete Sightings*. New York: Barnes & Noble, p. 54.

Byrne, Holt. 1966. "The Phantom of Flatwoods." *Sunday Gazette-Mail State Magazine* (Charleston, WV), March 6.

Figure 15.4. Split-image illustration compares fanciful Flatwoods Monster (left) with the real-world creature it most resembles, the common barn owl (right) (drawing by the author).

Clark, Jerome. 1998. *The UFO Encyclopedia*. 2nd ed. Detroit, MI: Omnigraphics, pp. 1:409–12.

Cloudsley-Thompson, John, et al. 1983. *Nightwatch: The Natural World from Dusk to Dawn*. New York: Facts on File.

Feschino, Frank C., Jr. 2004. *The Braxton County Monster Revealed*. Charleston, WV: Quarrier Press.

Keyhoe, Donald E. 1953. *Flying Saucers from Outer Space*. New York: Henry Holt.

Marchal, Terry. 1966. "Flatwoods Revisited." *Sunday Gazette-Mail State Magazine* (Charleston, WV), March 6.

May, Freddie. 2000. Telephone conversation with the author. June 12.

McGaha, James. 2006. Interview by the author. September 28–29. In Joe Nickell, "Mysterious Entities of the Pacific Northwest, Part II." *Skeptical Inquirer* 31, no. 2 (March/April 2007): 14–17.

"'Monster' Held Illusion Created by Meteor's Gas." 1952. *Charleston Gazette* (Charleston, WV), September 23.

Nickell, Joe, with John F. Fischer. 1992. *Mysterious Realms*. Amherst, NY: Prometheus Books.

Nickell, Joe. 2000. "The Flatwoods UFO Monster." *Skeptical Inquirer* 24, no. 6 (November/December): 15–19.

Peterson, Roger Tory. 1980. *A Field Guide to the Birds*. Boston, MA: Houghton Mifflin, pp. 174–75.

Ritchie, David. 1994. *UFO: The Definitive Guide to Unidentified Flying Objects and Related Phenomena*. New York: MJF Books, pp. 83, 96.

Sanderson, Ivan T. 1952. Typewritten report. Quoted in Byrne 1966 (above).

———. 1967. *Uninvited Visitors: A Biologist Looks at UFO's*. New York: Cowles, pp. 37–52.

Chapter 16
Attack of the "Little Green Men"

On the night of August 21, 1955, during the heyday of flying saucer reports, a western Kentucky family encountered—well, that is the question: What were the creatures that terrified a family at their farmhouse? What actually happened at Kelly, Kentucky, that evening?

For the fiftieth anniversary of the incident, I was invited to give a talk at a Little Green Men Festival in Hopkinsville, Kentucky, staged by its Chamber of Commerce. I determined to investigate the story that had caught the attention of the US Air Force's "Project Blue Book" (which investigated twelve thousand UFO reports from 1952 to 1969) and that also inspired a novel (Karyl 2004), a video documentary ("Monsters" 2005), and even an *X-Files* comic book ("Crop" 1997).

My investigation included visiting the site (see figure 16.1) in the company of UFOlogist and fellow invited speaker Peter Davenport. (We were each given a key to the city by Hopkinsville mayor Richard G. Liebe and chauffeured in his car on research jaunts by his driver, Rob Dollar.) I also obtained copies of original newspaper clippings at the Hopkinsville Public Library, conducted further research at the local museum, talked with witnesses to the events (see figure 16.2), studied detailed reports on the case, and much more (see figure 16.3). I even attended a Holiness Church tent revival, just down the road from the site of the Kelly incident, held in response to the Little Green Men Festival. Many of the congregation wore green T-shirts with the slogan "Son of Man Is Coming Back." Pastor Wendell "Birdie" McCord (2005) told me, "I don't know whether the green men is [*sic*] coming back, but I know the Son of Man is coming back."

Figure 16.1. Site of the 1955 Kelly, Kentucky, incident can still be seen (although the farmhouse has been replaced by a trailer) (photograph by the author).

Background

On the evening of Sunday, August 21, 1955, present at the Sutton farmhouse at Kelly were eleven people: widowed family matriarch Glennie Lankford (fifty); her children, Lonnie (twelve), Charlton (ten), and Mary (seven); two sons from her previous marriage, Elmer "Lucky" Sutton (twenty-five) and John Charley "J. C." Sutton (twenty-one), and their respective wives, Vera (twenty-nine) and Alene (twenty-seven); Alene's brother, O. P. Baker (around thirty or thirty-five); and a Pennsylvania couple, Billy Ray Taylor (twenty-one) and June Taylor (eighteen). The Taylors, along with "Lucky" and Vera Sutton, had been visiting for a while, being occasional carnival workers.

Not all of the eleven were eyewitnesses to the most significant events. One of the women, apparently June Taylor, had been "too frightened to look" (Davis and Bloecher 1978, 14), and Lonnie Lankford (2005), speaking to me at age 62, said that during the fracas his mother had hidden him and his brother and sister under a bed.

At about seven o'clock, Billy Ray Taylor was drawing water from the

Figure 16.2. Lonnie Lankford was only twelve years old when the "Little Green Men" incident occurred (photograph by the author).

Figure 16.3. The author is "kidnapped" by "aliens" at the fiftieth-anniversary festival of the incident in Kelly, Kentucky (author's photograph).

well when he saw a bright light streak across the sky and disappear beyond a tree line some distance from the house. According to researcher Isabel Davis, who investigated the case in 1956 (Davis and Bloecher 1978, 15), Billy Ray Taylor was different from the other eyewitnesses:

> He had looked at the creatures with extravagant success. He was the only member of the group who appeared to arouse immediate doubt in everyone who talked to him. . . . Even among the family he had a low standing; when he first came into the house and reported a "spaceship," they paid him no attention. Later, during the investigations, he basked in the limelight of publicity. He elaborated and embroidered his description of the creatures (though not his description of the "spaceship") and eventually produced the most imaginative and least credible of the little-men sketches. Several skeptics who labeled the story a hoax referred to him as the probable originator. His behavior was in sharp contrast to that of the other witnesses, none of whom aroused such prompt suspicion in the investigators.

About an hour after Taylor reported his "flying saucer" sighting, a barking dog attracted him and "Lucky" Sutton outside. Spotting a creature, they darted into the house for a .22 rifle and shotgun, thus beginning a series of encounters that spanned the next three hours. Sometimes, the men fired at a scary face that appeared at a window; sometimes, they went outside, whereupon, on one occasion, Taylor's hair was grabbed by a huge, clawlike hand. Once, the pair shot at a little creature that was on the roof and at another "in a nearby tree" that then "floated" to the ground. Either the creatures were impervious to gun blasts or the men's aim was poor, since no creature was killed.

After a lull in the "battle," everyone piled into their cars and drove eight miles south to Hopkinsville's police headquarters. Soon, more than a dozen officers—from city, county, and state law enforcement agencies—had converged on the site. Their search yielded nothing—apart from a hole in a window screen. There were "no tracks of 'little men,' nor was there any mark indicating anything had landed at the described spot behind the house." By the following day, the US Air Force was reportedly involved (Dorris 1955), but ultimately the case was listed as "unidentified" (Clark 1998).

Aliens?

The earliest articles on the incident did not refer to "little green men." That color was apparently later injected by the national media, although "Lucky" Sutton's son now says his father described them as "silver" with "a greenish silver glow" ("It Came" 2005, 8, 10).

Other details are also somewhat fuzzy. The beings were described in the first newspaper story as "about four feet tall," having "big heads" with "huge eyes" and "long arms" (Dorris 1955). However, they were downsized by Glennie Lankford (1955) to "two and a half feet tall" and were said to have large pointed ears, clawlike hands (with talons at the fingers' ends), and eyes that glowed (or shone) yellow. They also had "spindly," inflexible legs (Clark 1998; Davis and Bloecher 1978, 1, 28).

Although the earliest published story claims there were twelve to fifteen creatures, the fact is that in only one instance did the eyewitnesses see more than one creature, and that was the time (mentioned earlier) when a pair was spotted (one on the roof, one in a tree) (Clark 1998; Davis and Bloecher 1978, 18, 27).

From the outset, people offered their proposed solutions to the mystery. In addition to those who thought it was a hoax, some attributed the affair to alcohol intoxication. I talked with one of the original investigators, former Kentucky state trooper R. N. Ferguson (2005), who thought people there had been drinking, although he conceded he saw no evidence of that at the site. He told me he believed the monsters "came in a container" (i.e., a can or bottle of alcohol). A visitor to the farm the next day did notice "a few beer cans in a rubbish basket" (Davis and Bloecher 1978, 35). Whether or not drinking was involved, it was not responsible for the "saucer" sighting; other UFOs were witnessed in the area that evening (Davis and Bloecher 1978, 33). (More on this later.)

Monkeys represented another "theory." Supposedly, one or more monkeys had escaped either from a zoo or a traveling circus. However, there was never any credible evidence of such an escape (Clark 1998; Carlton 2005). The search for a terrestrial explanation of the incident would have to continue.

Solution

I long ago recognized the Kelly flap as being very similar to two alleged alien-encounter incidents that occurred in West Virginia, the 1952 appearance of

the "Flatwoods Monster" (chapter 15) and the 1966 "Mothman" sightings
—the first convincingly identified as a barn owl (Nickell 2000), the second as
a barred owl (Nickell 2002). (More about the Mothman in chapter 17.)

A year after my Flatwoods Monster article appeared in *Skeptical Inquirer*, a young French UFOlogist, Renaud Leclet, wrote articles on the Flatwoods and Kelly cases. He concurred with my determination in the former case, and now I can return the favor in the latter. I had suspected owls in the Kelly case, but—since I prefer to investigate on site—I was awaiting an opportunity to visit the area; that came with my invitation to speak at the event's fiftieth anniversary celebration. By then, Leclet had ventured to identify the Kelly entities from afar.

Although he and I have reached the same conclusion, he refers to the creature as an "eagle owl" (Leclet 2001), a designation for the genus *Bubo* that is not generally used by most authorities when specifically referring to the species Great Horned Owl (*Bubo virginianus*)—popularly called a "hoot owl." (See, for example, *National Audubon Society Field Guide to North American Birds: Eastern Region* [Bull and Ferrand 1994].) Confusion can thus occur.*

Echoing descriptions of the Kelly "little men," the Great Horned Owl has a height of some 25 inches; very large, staring, yellow eyes; long ear tufts; a large head, set (without apparent neck) on its shoulders; a light-grey underside; long wings that, seen on edge, could be mistaken for arms; spindly legs; claws with talons; and so on ("Great" 2006; Bull and Ferrand 1994). An owl could be on a roof or in a tree and be perceived to "float" to the ground. As to their behavior, Great Horned Owls are "extremely aggressive when defending the nest," and their activity typically "begins at dusk" ("Great" 2006).

Although some accounts claim that the little beings "glowed," Glennie Lankford, in her statement (1955), actually used the word *shining*. That might have been simply an effect caused by the farm lights.

As to the "flying saucer" sighting that preceded the encounter, there were area sightings of "meteors" at the time (Davis and Bloecher 1978, 33–34, 61–62). Most likely what was witnessed was a very bright meteor (or "fireball").

In summary, allowing for the heightened expectation prompted by the earlier "flying saucer" sighting, and for the effects of excitement and nighttime viewing, it seems likely that the famous 1955 Kelly incident is easily explained by a meteor and a pair of territorial owls.

What a hoot!

---

*For example, somehow Leclet (2001) reports "eagle owls" as having facial discs that are "white," whereas those of Great Horned Owls are yellow (or "tawny-buff": see "Great" 2006).

References

Bull, John, and John Ferrand Jr. 1994. *National Audubon Society Field Guide to North American Birds: Eastern Region.* New York: Alfred A. Knopf.

Carlton, Michelle. 2002. "Kelly Green Men: Children of Witness to Alleged Alien Invasion Defend Father's 1955 Claim." *Kentucky New Era* (Hopkinsville, KY), December 30.

——. 2005. "Myriad of Theories Speculate on Kelly Legend." In *It Came from Kelly* 2005, pp. 3, 14 (below).

Clark, Jerome. 1998. *UFO Encyclopedia.* 2nd ed. Detroit, MI: Omnigraphics, pp. 2:552–54.

Rozum, John. 1997. "Crop Duster." *X-Files* comic book 32. New York: Topps Comics. Cited in *It Came from Kelly* 2005, pp. 5, 12 (below).

Davis, Isabel, and Ted Bloecher. 1978. *Close Encounter at Kelly and Others of 1955.* Evanston, IL: Center for UFO Studies.

Dorris, Joe. 1955. "Story of Space Ship, 12 Little Men Probed Today." *Kentucky New Era* (Hopkinsville, KY), August 22. Cited in *It Came from Kelly* 2005, p. 10 (below).

Ferguson, R. N. 2005. Interview by the author.

"Great Horned Owl." 2006. The Owl Pages. http://www.owlpages.com/owls .php?genus=Bubo & species=virginianus (accessed July 7, 2006).

It Came from Kelly. 2005. Publication of *Kentucky New Era* newspaper (Hopkinsville, Kentucky), August.

Karyl, Anna. 2004. *The Kelly Incident.* Vallejo, CA: Gateway Publishers.

Lankford, Lonnie. 2005. Interview by the author. August 20.

Lankford, Glennie. 1955. Statement signed August 22. Text given in Davis and Bloecher 1978, p. 112 (above).

Leclet, Renaud. 2001. "Kelly-Hopkinsville." Series of articles dated August 28. http://francine.cordier.club.fr/pages/souspagekelly3eng.htm (accessed July 10, 2006).

McCord, Wendell. 2005. Interview by the author. August 19.

Monsters of the UFO. 2005. Video previewed August 20. Referenced in *It Came from Kelly* 2005, pp. 12–13 (above).

Nickell, Joe. 2000. "The Flatwoods UFO Monster." *Skeptical Inquirer* 24, no. 6 (November/December): 15–19.

——. 2002. "Mothman Revisited." *Skeptical Briefs* 12, no. 4 (December): 8–9.

Chapter 17
Mothman Metamorphosis

W hat began as an encounter with a strange creature near Point Pleasant, West Virginia, in 1966, soon turned into a "flap"— a series of sightings—that lasted from November 1966 to November 1967. It has since taken on mythic proportions, resulting in a book (Keel 1975) and 2002 movie, both titled *The Mothman Prophecies*. The creature has continued as the subject of paintings and sculptures (see figure 17.1), articles, chapters of books, and television documentaries, notably one for the History Channel's popular series *Monster Quest*, for which I was asked to take a fresh look at the Mothman phenomenon.

Background

The Mothman story began a few miles from Point Pleasant. It was late Tuesday night, November 15, 1966, when two couples were driving through an abandoned World War II munitions complex popularly called the TNT area. Suddenly, they saw a creature with fiercely red eyes— glowing, some would later say—walking with a shuffling gait. One witness stated that the creature was "shaped like a man, but bigger," adding "And it had big wings folded against its back." When it took flight it seemed to follow them although without "even flapping wings," yielding a mothlike or noiseless flight (quoted in Keel 1975, 59–63). The original witnesses have always insisted, despite longstanding rumors, that no drugs or alcohol were involved (Sergent and Warmsley 2002, 19, 55).

175

Figure 17.1. Mothman statue stands in downtown
Point Pleasant, West Virginia (author's photograph).

Soon others were seeing the winged creature. Two firemen visited the TNT area just three nights later and described the creature as "huge"; however, they insisted, "It was definitely a bird" (Keel 1975, 65). It was typically described as headless but with great eyes, shining red "like automobile reflectors," set near the top of its body. One woman, however, described it as having a "funny little face" along with those "big red poppy eyes" (Keel 1975, 71).

According to a popular legend of the area, "Mothman was nothing more than a prankster, a local man dressed in a Halloween costume who hid at the TNT site and jumped out at couples to frighten them. However, I investigated the case in Point Pleasant in mid-April 2002 and came to distrust the legend. Although there were *later* pranks—involving red flashlights tied to helium-filled balloons and even a "prankster pilot" (Nickell 2002)—the appearance of a costumed trickster is fundamentally incompatible with the original eyewitness descriptions of the creature, especially regarding the shining red eyes.

As ornithologists well know, some birds' eyes shine brightly at night when caught in a beam of light. One of the original eyewitnesses, Linda Scarberry (1966), emphasized that the effect was due to the car headlights. "There was no glowing about it until the lights hit it," she stated. Others echoed her statement. At another site, a man alerted by his dog aimed a flashlight toward his barn and saw "two red circles, or eyes, which looked like bicycle reflectors" (Keel 1975, 56).

As it happens, there is a winged creature with just such crimson eyeshine in the TNT area—which is part of the McClintic Wildlife Management Area, indeed a bird sanctuary! I refer to the barred owl (*Strix varia*)—a bird larger than a barn owl, which it somewhat resembles (hence the "funny little face"), exhibiting "strong" eyeshine. Very likely the Mothman sightings were caused by barred owls, as well as other types of owls. One was actually shot and killed during the Mothman flap (Nickell 2002a; 2002b) (see figure 17.2).

Owls are likely responsible for other birdman sightings, including the 1952 case of the Flatwoods Monster (Nickell 2000), and an entity appropriately called "Owlman" that sparked sightings in Cornwall, England, in 1976 (Coleman 2002, 34–36). Cryptozoologist Mark A. Hall (1998) has even suggested that Mothman may be a hitherto unknown species of giant owl! He dubs it "Bighoot." However, here is the question remaining: Which is more likely, that there is such an unknown creature or that encountering a frightening creature at night prompts some to misjudge its size?

Figure 17.2. This owl was shot by Asa Henry in November 1966, during the Mothman flap (photograph by the author).

In the Field

Seven years after my original Mothman investigation, at the invitation of the television show *Monster Quest*, I returned to Point Pleasant, West Virginia, to do further research and to conduct an experiment involving eyewitness testimony in such cases. While producer Anna Michelson handled myriad logistical matters, I worked with the film crew and a local artisan, Jan Haddox, to set up a test of people's perceptive ability when encountering something unfamiliar under unknown conditions. The basic idea was to see if they might misinterpret a fierce-eyed wild creature as being a much larger "monster."

Lacking trained barred owls who could jump out at test subjects on cue, I settled for something much less intense and, of course, less frightening: some Mothman cutouts. We prowled the area looking for a good test site and settled on an isolated one-lane roadway not far from the original 1966 sighting where we could drive a test subject past some installed monster cutouts. These were made in different sizes, each with a pair of round, bicycle-reflector eyes. An eight-foot-tall "monster" was placed 250 feet from the road, while a two-foot one was set at 100 feet and a four-foot cutout at just 85 feet.

The test was conducted on the night of August 27, 2009, from about nine to midnight. One at a time, test subjects were placed in a vehicle and driven down the lane while each "monster" in turn was briefly illuminated with a spotlight that caused the reflector "eyes" to shine. At the end of the run, I polled each subject and recorded his or her guesses as to the height of the cutouts together with their estimated distance from them. The results were, well, illuminating.

The estimated heights and distances varied wildly. The distances were estimated far too short (on average, the 250-foot distance was guessed at only 65.5 feet, while 100 was estimated at 74.8, and 85 at 42.4). The heights yielded better results, especially for the middle-sized (four-foot) figure, for which the average was exactly four feet! However, three persons guessed the smaller (two-foot) figure—the one closest to the size of a large owl—at twice its actual height.

This evidence thus shows that eyewitness accuracy varies, that estimates of distance and height of figures are untrustworthy, and that some guesses of height may be exaggerated by 100 percent, possibly more. It would seem that an actual frightening creature in motion would be more likely to be exaggerated as to height.

Indeed, something that is frightening looms large in one's consciousness. Moreover, an expert in the distortion of memory at the University of Minnesota, Chad Marsolek (who appeared with me on the *Monster Quest* program), described a "weapon-focus effect" which can cause an eyewitness, focusing on something frightening (the barrel of a gun, for example), to lose focus on other elements. Interestingly, when people view a disturbing image they tend to be confident of their accuracy—even when their memory is wrong (Marsolek 2010).

Iconography

An important aspect of the Mothman legend is its iconography—how its appearance is represented. A study of the Mothman case shows that its image has evolved over time. At the beginning, for example, in 1966, the creature debuted with those large shining eyes—as "two bright red circles"—set near the top of its otherwise headless body, together with folding wings (Keel 1975, 52–63; Sergent and Wamsley 2002, 16). At this stage—except for its size—the creature's description is consistent with its having been a barred owl (Nickell 2002b).

Following its initial TNT-area sighting, the supposedly man-sized creature was dubbed "Mothman"—a newspaper spin-off from the comic character Batman, then popular as a television series. With "man" now part of its moniker, the entity would in time sprout arms as it morphed in the popular imagination into a man-beast. Now, nature produces some creatures with wings and others with arms (or forelegs), but never with both—although mythology offers many examples (including some representations of fairies [Bord 1997], gargoyles, and other entities [Conway 2002]). Over time, the arms—absent from the earliest accounts and the first eyewitness drawing (Sergent and Wamsley 2002, 16)—would be "remembered" by eyewitnesses. Linda Scarberry has since stated (in Sergent and Wamsley 2002, 27), "I could see the muscles in the arms and legs of the Mothman," even though in 1966 she had written, "I couldn't see its head or arms" (quoted in Sergent and Wamsley 2002, 51).

Since 2003, an eleven-foot-tall, stainless-steel effigy of Mothman commands attention in downtown Point Pleasant (see figure 17.1) ("Mothman Statue" 2009). It is a much different creature from the "man-sized, bird-like creature" that was initially reported in the *Point Pleasant Register* of November 16, 1966 (clipping reproduced in Sergent and Wamsley 2002, 68–70). Having acquired arms and a now distinctly humanoid body, the entity has been further transformed into an extraterrestrial-type being. Its original round, owl-like eyes have been changed to an almond-shaped, wraparound form common to some depictions of aliens, with evocation of a 1983 "Lizard Man" type (Huyghe 1996, 82–83). The monster even resembles a version of the currently legendary creature called the "Chupacabra"—itself now sometimes being portrayed as a red-eyed, alienesque entity (see Nickell 2004, 29) (compare figure 17.1 with 13.1).

As it evolves in popular culture—the subject, for example, of an ill-fated Hollywood movie in 2002—Mothman takes its place among the fantastic creatures of our imagination, definitely a variety of man-beast. As one source observes, "Mothman . . . is more than a monster—he's a celebrity" ("Mothman Statue" 2009).

References

Bord, Janet. 1997. *Fairies: Real Encounters with Little People.* New York: Carroll & Graf.

Coleman, Loren. 2002. *Mothman and Other Curious Encounters.* New York: Paraview Press.

Conway, D. J. 2002. *Magical, Mystical Creatures.* St. Paul, MN: Llewellyn Publications.

Hall, Mark A. 1998. "Bighoot—The Giant Owl." *Wonders* 5, no. 3 (September): 67–79. Cited in Coleman 2002 (above).

Keel, John A. 1975. *The Mothman Prophecies.* Reprinted; New York: Tor, 1991.

Marsolek, Chad. 2010. *Monster Quest* episode aired on History, February 10.

"Mothman Statue." 2009. Roadside American. http://www.roadsideamerica.com/story/12036 (accessed August 31, 2009).

Nickell, Joe. 2000. "The Flatwoods UFO Monster." *Skeptical Inquirer* 24, no. 6, (November/December): 15–19.

———. 2002a. "'Mothman' Solved!" *Skeptical Inquirer* 26, no. 2 (March/April): 20–21.

———. 2002b. "Mothman Revisited: Investigating on Site." *Skeptical Briefs* 12, no. 4 (December): 8–9.

———. 2004. *The Mystery Chronicles: More Real-Life X-Files.* Lexington, KY: University Press of Kentucky.

Scarberry, Linda. 1966. Handwritten account reproduced in Sergent and Wamsley 2002, pp. 36–59 (below).

Sergent, Dorrie, Jr., and Jeff Wamsley. 2002. *Mothman: The Facts behind the Legend.* Point Pleasant, WV: Mothman Lives Publishing.

Chapter 18

The Humanoids

O ver time, diverse aliens like those we have seen thus far—such as the winged Mothman, and the diminutive, goblinesque Kelly entities—began to give way to increasingly humanoid-appearing varieties. They are products not of Darwinian-type evolution but rather of the evolution of an idea in popular culture. Here we look first at some gigantic humanoids (including one reminiscent of the Cyclops, the one-eyed giants of Greek mythology); then we look at how the now-standard alien likeness developed, how it featured in a famous "alien autopsy" film, and how the Roswell saga became the Holy Grail of UFOlogy.

Humanoid Giants

Some of the alien humanoids were of monstrous proportions. One such being was described by three boys, two aged seven and another twelve, in Belo Horizonte, Brazil, in 1969. They claimed to have seen a spherical UFO hovering nearby and, through its transparent shell, spied four beings. One, about ten feet tall, floated to the ground dressed in a diving suit and clear helmet, through which the boys could see that it possessed a single, large, dark eye. When the cyclopean entity approached them, gesturing and speaking strange words, the older boy lifted a brick threateningly. The giant sent forth a beam that knocked the brick from the boy's hand, then levitated back into the sphere, which silently rose and vanished. Later, tri-

183

angular markings were found on the path where the cyclopean giant had stridden.

The tale has largely passed into obscurity, except for its inclusion in a book devoted to the myriad descriptions of extraterrestrials (Huyghe 1996, 54–55). Few seem to have taken it seriously, probably having been unable to distinguish the alleged encounter from a hoax—a possibility illuminated by the next case.

From 1989 in Voronezh, Russia, comes the report of another ten-foot-tall being who emerged from a hovering spherical craft. Wearing silver coveralls, the giant had three eyes. When the forty or so witnesses began shouting, the entity vanished along with the sphere, only to reappear five minutes later. The being pointed a four-foot tube at a teenage boy, causing him to disappear. However, after the entity reentered the craft and it flew away, the teenager reappeared. What to make of this monster? According to Patrick Huyghe (1996, 52):

> Some witnesses reported having seen a symbol, known as UMMO, on the being's belt and on the object. This design had been reported in several close encounters in Spain during the 1970s. Most investigators believe it was all a clever hoax by a small cult claiming contact with an extraterrestrial civilization. A report on UFO shapes, which had been published in Voronezh, had included the UMMO symbol, and investigators believed that this had contaminated an otherwise solid case.

Alien Likeness

The concept of what alien creatures look like has undergone change over time, like other evolved images, such as Jesus's features in art (Nickell 1988, 41–48), or of the popular likeness of Santa Claus in pop culture (Flynn 1993).

The development begins with the modern UFO era in 1947. A great variety of alien types were described in the post-1947 era (Clark 1993a; Cohen 1982; Hendry 1979; Huyghe 1996; Lorenzen and Lorenzen 1977; Mack 1994; McCampbell 1976; Sachs 1980; Stringfield 1977, 1980; Story 1980; Vallee 1969). There were "little green men" supposedly encountered in Italy in 1947 (Cohen 1982, 203–205); humanlike beings bathed in light who appeared to 1950s "contactees" (Story 1980, 89); "hairy dwarfs" reported in 1954 (Clark 1993a, 177); and many other extraterrestrials reportedly encountered. Figure 18.1 shows a selection of such beings from 1947 to the present. (Science fiction examples have not been included.)

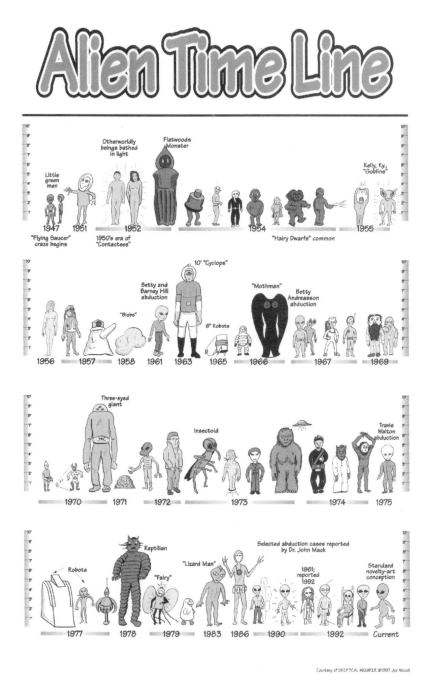

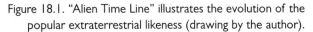

Figure 18.1. "Alien Time Line" illustrates the evolution of the popular extraterrestrial likeness (drawing by the author).

This Alien Timeline appeared on a Discovery channel program on alien abductions, and also on ABC's *20/20* (April 4, 1997) in a documentary on the "Alien Autopsy" hoax (discussed in the next section). The aliens depicted in the film were of a type not popularly conceived until years later.

That alien model began to appear after the first widely reported alien abduction—the Betty and Barney Hill case in 1961. It is a humanoid with a small body, a big head, and large, wraparound eyes. This type seems to represent *us* as it is assumed we *will be* in our remote evolutionary future (Nickell 1984). Thus, such aliens have dwindling bodies but large brains (due to inactivity coupled with increased intelligence). However, there is reason to be skeptical of all such humanlike models. As one early commentator states: "While it seems incredible that life does not exist elsewhere in the universe, it is equally incredible that it should resemble man" (Palmer 1951, 64).

Still, due to the influence of popular media, this is the type that eventually won out. It is the standardized alien image, now seen everywhere (see figure 18.2.)

Figure 18.2. Alien toys and novelties show standardization of the depiction in popular culture (author's photograph).

"Alien Autopsy" Film

Britain's *Manchester Evening News* termed it a hoax that "fooled the world" (Salford 2006). Well, not exactly: *Skeptical Inquirer* magazine was on to the 1995 "Alien Autopsy" film from the outset.* But now the reputed creator of the fake extraterrestrial corpse used for the "autopsy" has publicly confessed.

The film—purporting to depict the postmortem of an extraterrestrial that died in a UFO crash at Roswell, New Mexico, in mid 1947 (see figure 18.3)—was part of a "documentary" that aired on the Fox television network. Skeptics and many UFOlogists quickly branded the affair a hoax.

Among numerous observations, they noted that the film bore a bogus, nonmilitary codemark, that the injuries sustained by the extraterrestrial were inconsistent with an air crash, and that the person performing the autopsy held the scissors like a tailor rather than a pathologist (who is trained to place his middle or ring finger in the bottom of the scissors hole

Figure 18.3. Scene from *Alien Autopsy* television program purports to show the postmortem of an extraterrestrial from the Roswell "UFO crash" (photograph courtesy of the *Skeptical Inquirer* science magazine).

*My article on the case (Nickell 1995) inaugurated my column, "Investigative Files," in *Skeptical Inquirer*.

and use his forefinger to steady the blades). Houston pathologist Ed Uthman (1995) faulted the film for lacking what he aptly termed "technical verisimilitude."

Other pathologists agreed. Cyril Wecht (1995), former president of the National Association of Forensic Pathologists, described the viscera in terms that could apply to supermarket meat scraps: "I cannot relate these structures to abdominal context." Nationally known pathologist Dominick Demaio (1995) was even more succinct: "I would say it's a lot of bull."

Hollywood special-effects expert Trey Stokes (whose film credits include *The Blob, Batman Returns,* and *Tales from the Crypt*) told *Skeptical Inquirer* that the alien corpse behaved like a dummy, seeming lightweight, "rubbery," and therefore moving unnaturally when handled (Stokes 1995).

Belatedly, a Manchester sculptor and special-effects creator, John Humphreys, now claims that the Roswell alien was his handiwork, and that it was destroyed after the film was shot. He made the revelation just as a new movie, *Alien Autopsy,* was being released, a film for which he re-created the original creature. Released in April 2006, it retells the making of the 1995 hoax autopsy film, with a pair of British television celebrities playing the original producers, Ray Santilli and Gary Shoefield. Santilli now claims that the 1995 film was a re-creation of genuine footage that became damaged when its container was opened after forty-eight years (Horne 2006). It's hard to imagine anyone believing him.

As Humphreys told the BBC, "Funnily enough, I used exactly the same process as before. You start with the stills from the film, blow them up as large as you can. Then you make an aluminum armature, which you cover in clay, and then add all the detail." The clay model was used to produce a mold that yielded a latex cast. The body cavities were filled, Humphreys admitted, with chicken entrails, sheep brains, and the like, which were purchased from a meat market near the north London flat in which the film was shot (Horne 2006).

Are Humphreys's claims credible? Indeed, not only is he a graduate of the Royal Academy and a special-effects model-maker—his credits include *Max Headroom* and *Doctor Who*—but his re-creations are so good as to leave no doubt of his ability to have made the originals. And examples of his work displayed on his Web site (Humphreys 2006) are stylistically consistent with the hoaxed aliens.

Humphreys also admitted that in the original autopsy film, he himself played the role of the pathologist; his identity was concealed by a contamination suit.

Roswell Saga

The alien autopsy hoax represented the culmination of several years' worth of rumors, urban legends, and outright deceptions, purporting to prove that saucer wreckage and the remains of its humanoid occupants were stored at a secret facility—e.g., a (nonexistent) "Hangar 18" at Wright Patterson Air Force Base—and that the small corpses were autopsied at that or another site.

Among the hoaxes were the following:

- A 1949 science-fiction movie, *The Flying Saucer*, purported to contain scenes of a captured spacecraft; an actor actually posed as an FBI agent and swore the claim was true.
- In 1950, writer Frank Scully reported in his *Behind the Flying Saucers* that the US government possessed no fewer than three Venusian spaceships, together with the humanoid corpses found on board. Scully had been fed the tale by two confidence men who had hoped to sell a petroleum locating device allegedly based on alien technology (Clark 1993b).
- In 1974, Robert Spencer Carr began to promote one of the crashes from the Scully book and to claim firsthand knowledge of where the pickled aliens were stored. But as the late claimant's son told *Skeptical Inquirer* readers (Carr 1997), Carr was a spinner of yarns who made up the entire story.
- In 1987, the author of a book on Roswell released the notorious "MJ-12 documents," which seemed to prove the crash-retrieval story and a high-level government coverup. Unfortunately, document experts readily exposed the papers as inept forgeries (Nickell 1995; Nickell and Fischer 1990).
- In 1990, Gerald Anderson claimed that he and family members had been rock hunting in the New Mexico desert in 1947, when they came upon a crashed saucer with injured aliens among the still-burning wreckage. Anderson released a diary his uncle had purportedly kept that recorded the event. Alas, forensic tests showed that the ink used to write the entries had not been manufactured until 1974 (Nickell 2001, 120).

The most elaborate Roswell hoax, however, and the one that probably reached the largest audience, was the "Alien Autopsy" film. It will be remembered as a classic of the genre. The truth about "the Roswell incident"—that the crash device was merely a secret US spy balloon, part of Project Mogul, which attempted to monitor emissions from anticipated Soviet nuclear tests—continues to be obscured by hoaxers, conspiracy cranks, and hustlers.

We should again recall Paul Kurtz's statement at the time of the original film's airing: "The Roswell myth should be permitted to die a deserved death. Whether or not we are alone in the universe will have to be decided on the basis of better evidence than that provided by the latest bit of Roswell fakery" (Nickell 1995, 19).

References

Clark, Jerome. 1993a. *Unexplained*. Detroit, MI: Visible Ink.

Carr, Timothy Spencer. 1997. "Son of Originator of 'Alien Autopsy' Story Casts Doubt on Father's Credibility." *Skeptical Inquirer* 21, no. 4 (July/August): 31–32.

———. 1993b. "UFO Hoaxes." In *Encyclopedia of Hoaxes*, ed. Gordon Stein, 267–78. Detroit, MI: Gale Research.

Cohen, Daniel. 1982. *The Encyclopedia of Monsters*. New York: Dorsett Press.

Damaio, Dominick. 1995. Appearance on American Journal, September 6.

Films. 2006. BBC Homepage, April 18. Available at www.bbc.co.uk/manchester/content/articles/2006/04/07070406_alien_interview_features.html (accessed April 18, 2006).

Flynn, Tom. 1993. *The Trouble with Christmas*. Amherst, NY: Prometheus Books.

Hendry, Allan. 1979. *The UFO Handbook*. New York: Doubleday.

Horne, Marc. 2006. "'Max Headroom' Creator Made Roswell Alien." *Sunday Times*. April 16. http://www.timesonline.co.uk/article/0,,2087-2136617,00 .html (accessed April 25, 2006).

Humphreys, John. 2006. Official website: http://www.john-humphreys.com/index.html (accessed April 18, 2006).

Huyghe, Patrick. 1996. *The Field Guide to Extraterrestrials*. New York: Avon Books.

Lorenzen, Coral, and Jim Lorenzen. 1977. *Abducted: Confrontations with Beings from Outer Space*. New York: Berkeley Medallion Books.

Mack, John. 1994. *Abduction*. New York: Ballantine.

McCampbell, James M. 1976. *UFOLOGY: A Major Breakthrough in the Scientific Understanding of Unidentified Flying Objects*. Millbrae, CA: Celestial Arts.

Nickell, Joe. 1984. "The 'Hangar 18' Tales: A Folkloristic Approach." *Common Ground*, June.

———. 1988. *Inquest on the Shroud of Turin*. Updated ed. Amherst, NY: Prometheus Books.

———. 1995. "Alien Autopsy Hoax." *Skeptical Inquirer* 19, no. 6 (November/December): 17–19.

———. 2001. *Real-Life X-Files: Investigating the Paranormal.* Lexington, KY: University Press of Kentucky.

Nickell, Joe, and John F. Fischer. 1990. "The Crashed-Saucer Forgeries." *International UFO Reporter* (March/April): 4–12.

Palmer, R. 1951. "New Report on the Flying Saucers." *Fate* (January): 63–81.

Sachs, Margaret. 1980. *The UFO Encyclopedia.* New York: Perigree Books.

"Salford Man Admits Alien Autopsy Fake." 2006. *Manchester Evening News.* April 6. http://www.manchesteronline.co.uk/men/news/showbiz/s/210/21 (accessed April 6, 2006).

———. 1980. *The UFO Crash/Retrieval Syndrome.* Seguin, TX: Mufon.

Stokes, Trey. 1995. Personal communications with Barry Karr. August 29–31; cited in Nickell 1995, "Alien Autopsy Hoax."

Story, Ronald D. 1980. *The Encyclopedia of UFOs.* Garden City, NY: Doubleday.

Stringfield, Leonard H. 1977. *Situation Red: The UFO Siege.* Garden City, NY: Doubleday.

Uthman, Ed. 1995. "Fox's 'Alien Autopsy': A Pathologist's View." Usenet. September 15.

Vallee, Jacques. 1969. *Passport to Magonia: From Folklore to Flying Saucers.* Chicago, IL: Henry Regnery.

Wecht, Cyril. 1995. Quoted on "Alien Autopsy: Fact or Fiction?" Fox Network, August 28 and September 4.

Chapter 19
Unidentified Flying Humanoids

Beginning in March 2000, sightings of a relatively new type of UFO—or rather, UFH: "unidentified flying humanoid"—have been reported. Seen in scant locations—notably Mexico and the western United States—these are floating objects that some eyewitnesses perceive as dark, humanlike entities ("Terror" 2009). I was asked by History's popular television show *Monster Quest* to look into the reported phenomenon.

Sightings

The first occurrence was in Mexico, in Colonia Agricola Oriental, in March 2000, and the object was videotaped by a man named Salvador Guerrero. Then, in December of the same year, Guerrero filmed another *hombrecito voladero* ("little flying man") at the same location—thus making him what is known in skeptical parlance as a "repeater." Moreover, Guerrero not only experienced the equivalent of lightning striking twice but happened to have a video camera both times ("Mysterious" 2005). This seems fortuitous indeed.

Other videotaped occurrences come from near Monterrey, Mexico (where an emotional police officer allegedly suffered an "attack"—perhaps by a "witch," he said—in 2002), as well as from Cuernavaca and Mexico City. From the United States come videos as well. One was made by Ed Sherwood (2006), a crop circle "investigator," who acknowledges that "remarkably, less than four months after viewing the video evidence from Mexico," he and his wife "observed something nearly identical fly over our neighborhood near our apartment, and I managed to film it!" Exclamation point indeed! Another video was made by Rich Giordano of Phoenix, described as a "Skywatcher/UFOlogist" who states, "I have taped several hours of unexplained lights, formations and humanoid type UFOs and have familiarized myself with the history of UFOs simultaneously." He adds, "I am no different then [sic] you except that I videotape UFOs" (Giordano 2010a).

Typically, the dark objects have a vaguely humanoid form. However, they are wingless and appear to remain in a fixed, standing position while moving horizontally. They "hover," "glide," "spin," and "float," consistent with light, wind-borne objects ("Terror" 2009; Yturria 2005).

The new UFHs are therefore different from previously reported ones like the Flatwoods Monster (Nickell 2001, 301–310), Mothman (Nickell 2004, 93–99), and the Kelly, Kentucky, "goblins" or "little green men" (Nickell 2006; Huyghe 1996, 84), which were winged entities that were animated and not merely drifting. Most nonwinged humanoids from the sky arrive in flying saucers or other purportedly extraterrestrial craft (Huyghe 1996), although some are said to be able to float to and from their hovering spaceships (e.g., Huyghe 1996, 54–55).

Analysis

Monster Quest had a law enforcement video analyst examine various video sequences depicting UFHs. The expert found one of the objects to be moving as if along a cable, thus discrediting its supposed identification as a UFH. As to others, he concluded that the visual data was too poor to allow definitive analysis. The videos themselves did not appear to have been Photoshopped or otherwise faked, but the analyst stated pointedly that that did not mean they were not unfaked videos of "constructed" scenes, possibly "balloon" in nature. (One object's seemingly emitting light was instead probably only reflecting the morning sun.) ("Terror" 2009) Other analysts (commissioned by the Discovery Channel), who examined the Giordano video, concluded that what it depicted was "probably balloons," and they did a re-creation, videotaping a balloon cluster (Giordano 2009; 2010b). I went on to develop the balloon hypothesis more fully, observing that some sequences—notably a 2004 Santa Monica video—show an object that clearly has round composite elements suggestive of a balloon cluster.

Experimentation

For *Monster Quest*, I attempted to replicate the phenomenon, choosing for my demonstration clusters of dark, helium-filled balloons. These were assembled outside the Montreal offices of the TV production company contracted to *Monster Quest*, where they were then released and video-taped. When the balloons were only held together by their strings, they tended to separate, losing their bulk form. However, when they were held together with tape, the effect was a convincing re-creation of a UFH. Center for Inquiry video expert Tom Flynn captured a frame from the video of a typical UFH, made at Santa Monica in 2004, and a frame from a *Monster Quest* video of one of my experimental balloon clusters.

As shown in figure 19.1, the appearance of the questioned video's UFH is consistent with a balloon cluster. Indeed, an experimental balloon cluster convincingly simulates the effect (again, see figure 19.1), leading me to conclude that at least some of the UFHs are, at best, misidentifications, and, at worst, deliberate hoaxes by persons unknown.

References

Giordano, Rich. 2009. "Discovery Channel's *X-Testers* Attempts to Debunk 'Flying Humanoid.'" http://www.ufocasebook.com/xtesters.html (accessed April 3, 2009).

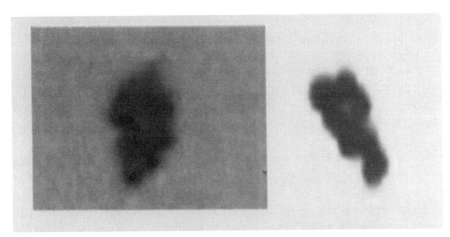

Figure 19.1. An "unidentified flying humanoid" (left) is compared with a cluster of balloons (right), showing obvious similarity (stills from a *Monster Quest 2009* documentary).

————. 2010a. Appearance on Fastwalkers. http://www.fastwalkers.com/featured/RichGiordano.htm (accessed March 18, 2010).

————. 2010b. "Trying to Debunk the Humanoids." http://www.cnufos.com/hdr.htm (accessed March 18, 2010).

Nickell, Joe. 2001. *Real-Life X-Files: Investigating the Paranormal.* Lexington, KY: University Press of Kentucky, pp. 301–10.

————. 2004. *The Mystery Chronicles: More Real-Life X-Files.* Lexington, KY: University Press of Kentucky, pp. 93–99.

————. 2006. "Siege of 'Little Green Men': The 1955 Kelly, Kentucky, Incident." *Skeptical Inquirer* 30, no. 6 (December): 12–14.

Sherwood, Ed. 2006. "An Unidentified 'Flying Humanoid' Videotaped above Santa Monica?" http://www.cropcircleanswers.com/FlyingHumanoid.htm (accessed March 18, 2010).

"Terror from the Skies." 2009. *Monster Quest,* History television documentary aired July 29.

Yturria, Santiago. 2005. "The Mysterious Flying Humanoids." http://www.rense.com/general66/humsan.htm (accessed April 3, 2009).

Part 5

Manimals

Chapter 20

Hybrids

Among legendary man-beasts are those creatures that supposedly "combine human and animal forms in one body." They have been termed "semihominid hybrids" or simply "manimals," according to the cryptozoological book titled *A Natural History of the Unnatural World* (Levy 1999, 110).

Since the term is applied to creatures that are not known to exist, any taxonomy (classification) is necessarily nonscientific. Although some would include among manimals the werewolf, I use *manimal* here to refer only to those alleged man–animal creatures that have a distinctive, yoked-together appearance. They are generally of two types: creatures having animal heads with human bodies, such as the minotaur, and those with human upper portions and animal bodies, like the centaur (and merpeople, who deserve their own chapter.)

Animal-headed Humans

The ancients often represented their deities and other mythological creatures as men who possessed the heads of animals. The Egyptians, for instance, worshiped the sun god Horus (the son of Osiris and Isis) who was represented as a falcon-headed man.

Hindu mythology likewise has a bird-man in the form of the semi-deistic Garuda, who possesses a human body and limbs but has the head, wings, and claws of a gigantic eagle. Kind and benevolent, Garuda serves as both steed and servant to Vishnu, one of the most important of the Hindu gods (Conway 2002, 81).

Similarly, one of the aspects of the Indian god Vishnu is the Man-Lion. Depicted in carvings and sculptures as a four-armed man with a lion's head, he represents the half-tame, half-fierce nature that is within all creatures—including humans (Conway 2002, 110).

In the Hindu pantheon are also the *Gandharvas* (or "Fragrances"), described in the *Atharva-veda* as shaggy, half-animal entities. They are often depicted with a human body topped with the head of a horse (or occasionally a bird). Said to be mates of woodland nymphs, they are portrayed even in today's masquerades as lustful horse-men who represent nature's fecundity (Leach 1984, 440; Conway 2002, 44).

In the ancient Middle Eastern empires, as early as the third millennium BCE, were depicted bull-headed men, sometimes shown in combat with human heroes. The best-known of such creatures is the Greek monster, the Minotaur, whose name comes from the Greek *Minos*, King of Crete, and *taurus*, bull).

In Greek mythology,

> Minos offered to sacrifice the white bull sent from the sea by Poseidon, but instead sacrified another. Poseidon therefore incited lust in Pasiphae, Minos' queen, for the white bull. The craftsman Daedalus made a hollow wooden form, covered it with a cow's hide, and placed Pasiphae within it. In this manner the queen was able to indulge her passion; the resulting offspring was Asterius, the Minotaur. Some years later, Androgeus, a son of Minos, having won at the Panathenaic games, was waylaid and slain by a group of jealous Athenians. Minos marched on Athens and forced from them a tribute of seven youths and seven maidens every ninth year, to be shut up in the Labyrinth to be eaten by the Minotaur. With the third such group went Theseus, son of Ægeus, king of Athens. He slew the Minotaur with his fists and thus ended the practice of sending the youthful sacrifice to Crete.

The story is thought to reflect the bull and sun cult of Crete, with Theseus's victory representing an end to the Greek practice of sacrificing humans to the sun (Leach 1984, 729).

Human-headed Animals

Among the hybrids in which the animal-man components are reversed is the familiar Sphinx of Egypt. Its image stood before temples, combining a man's head with a lion's body. Its most familiar example is the great stone monument near the pyramids, nearly seventy feet high and more than two hundred feet long. Badly eroded, it was damaged during the Islamic conquest when a Moslem fanatic, viewing it as an abominable idol, broke off its nose (Conway 2002, 131).

The Greeks had a variety of such mythological hybrids, including a sphinx, although it had a female head and wings. Sent by Hera as a plague on the city of Thebes, the monster killed all who were unable to answer its riddle: "What animal walks on four feet in the morning, on two at noon, and on three in the evening?" Oedipus correctly replied, "Man, who crawls on all fours at the beginning of his life, then walks on two feet, and needs the help of a cane at the end of his life." Thereupon the sphinx killed herself (Hendricks 1963, 139; Benét's 1987, 924).

Among other Greek hybrid entities were the fierce centaurs, who were half human and half stallion. As Daniel Cohen observes in his *Super-Monsters* (1977, 99):

> There is no real centaur, and there never was. But the myth is based on something. That something is the mounted nomads that from time to time swept down on Greek-controlled lands. In very early times the Greeks did not ride horses. They only used donkeys or horses to pull carts. The first time the Greeks actually saw people riding horses, they must have been astonished. The nomads rode very well. It looked as though horse and rider were two parts of the same creature. That is how the legend of the centaur must have begun.

This effect is shown in figure 20.1.

Similarly, there were the satyrs, woodland deities whose lower half was that of a goat. The latter were followers of Pan, the god of the countryside who was depicted as a bearded, snub-nosed man with the legs, horns, and ears of a goat. A fertility figure, he wandered through the woods while playing music on a reed pipe (Hendricks 1963, 114, 134; Benét's 1987, 171, 733, 869; Conway 2002, 51–58).

Then there were the sirens (from the Greek *seiren*, "entangler"). These were mythical monsters, whose irresistible singing lured sailors to their destruction. They were generally depicted as having a woman's head and the body and wings of a bird. According to one legend, they were com-

Figure 20.1. In *The Centaur*, a bronze statue by Charles Gary Rumsey (1879–1922), horse and man seem one (photograph by the author at the Buffalo Historical Society).

panions of the spring goddess Persephone and, when she was abducted by Hades to become his queen of the Lower World, they searched for her. However, in some later traditions sirens were depicted as mermaids (Levy 1999, 114–115).

Other creatures with the faces of women and bodies of birds were the Harpies, but they were most unsirenlike. Their name is from the Greek *harpyiai* "snatchers," and they were hideous, vulturelike monsters that seized victims' food and carried out other torments. According to one source (*Benét's* 1987, 426), "They seem to have combined the primitive concept of wind spirits and predatory ghosts with actual characteristics of carrion birds." Levy (1999, 115) cautions that "writers and artists have often used the terms Siren, harpy, and mermaid interchangeably." (See, for instance, the siren–mermaid creature in figure 20.2: We know it is intended as a harpy because it visually puns by forming the front portion of the frame of a harp.)

Before we turn to merpeople in the next chapter, we should look at their reptilian counterparts. These include the Greek demi-god Achelous, the river deity. Depicted as a horned man from the waist up and with a serpent's lower body, he ruled over Greece's largest river until he was defeated by Heracles, his rival for the love of a human maiden.

Figure 20.2. Sometimes a Harpy was depicted as sirenlike
(from an 1832 catalog of printers' type and devices).

Other serpent-people are the one thousand Nagas, semi-divine offspring of the Hindu goddess Kadru. (*Naga* is from the Hindu *nag*,
"snake," as is *Naja*, the genus of snakes of the family *Najidae*. The name
Nagas also describes a historical snake-worshipping people of trans-
Himalayan origin.) The mythological Nagas are usually depicted with
human heads on cobra bodies. Their forehead or throat carries a magical
jewel that provides them with supernatural power over all water (Conway
2002, 115–17, 120–23; Leach 1984, 780).

Exhibited Hybrids

Not all hybrid monsters are confined to the realm of mythology. Some are real enough to display in carnival sideshows (like the exhibited "freaks" of chapter 1 and the midway wild men of chapter 4).

Among notable sideshow hybrids are the "alligator" boys and girls (afflicted with the scaly skin condition ichthyosis), "leopard" people (dark-skinned persons with vitiligo, a lack of pigmentation that can appear as a pattern of white splotches), various "frog" boys (who might have any of a number of deformities such as diminished legs), "seal" people (with missing limbs and hands and feet that are attached to the trunk), "lobster" folk (whose hands and feet have some digits missing while the others are fused into opposed "claws"), and others (Nickell 2005, 80–150).

Not only were such oddities imaginatively interpreted in manimalistic terms, but they were often depicted on their sideshow banners in exaggerated fashion, commonly with a human head and torso and an animal's body. For instance, in 1969, when I worked as a pitchman on the midway of the Canadian National Exhibition, I met El Hoppo the Living Frog Boy. His banner depicted him as a youth with a frog's hindquarters. In reality, "Hoppy" was a grey-bearded man in a wheelchair who had spindly limbs and a distended stomach. To make him more closely resemble his amphibianesque banner image, he was stripped to the waist and dressed in green tights (Nickell 2005, 146–47).

Exhibited hybrids were not only enhanced but were often "gaffed" (faked) as well, as noted in earlier chapters. For example, an "alligator" person could be simulated by painting a willing carny's exposed body with tinted casein glue and, after it dried, having him or her twist and flex to help create the cracking pattern that simulates genuine ichthyosis. Among other gaffed hybrids were Koo-Koo the Bird Girl and Lionella the Lion-Faced Girl (Nickell 2005, 194–202).

Some of the gaffed oddities—like Spidora (a supposed spider-girl), certain "snake girls," and a "human butterfly"—are actually classed as illusions. The usual presentation involves a real young lady, a means (such as a mirror) of concealing all but her head, and the fake giant body of an aracnid, serpent, or other animal of choice. This body may contain coil springs or the like, so as to be secretly moved to impart seeming life to the model (Nickell 2005, Blanchan 278–282).

Finally, there are preserved exhibits. Along with such fakes as a frozen Sasquatch (chapter 8) and devil men (chapter 14), gaffed hybrids take their place. Most are animal-animal combinations like the "jackalope," an example of the taxidermist's art—in this case a jackrabbit fitted with ante-lope antlers. Of the animal–human genre, none are more widespread—or more infamous—than the supposedly preserved (but actually gaffed) spec-imens of mermaids that we investigate presently. But first we must look at the "real" variety.

References

Benét's Reader Encyclopedia. 1987. 3rd ed. New York: Harper & Row.

Cohen, Daniel. 1977. *Super-Monsters.* New York: Archway (Pocket Books).

Conway, D. J. 2002. *Magical, Mystical Creatures.* St. Paul, MN: Llewellyn Publi-cations.

Hendricks, Rhoda A. 1963. *Mythology Pocket Crammer.* New York: Ken Pub-lishing.

Leach, Maria, ed. 1984. *Funk & Wagnalls Standard Dictionary of Folklore, Mythology, and Legend.* New York: Harper & Row.

Levy, Joel, ed. 1999. *A Natural History of the Unnatural World.* New York: St. Martin's Press.

Chapter 21

Merpeople

Among Earth's remote regions, the seas are said to offer sanctuaries for fabled creatures—not only sea serpents but merpeople as well. In this chapter we examine the folk traditions and look at Barnum's Fejee Mermaid and other fakes.

Merfolk

The Middle Ages saw widespread belief in the mermaid (after the Middle English words *mer*, "sea," and *maide*, short for maiden, meaning "an unmarried girl or woman"). According to *Funk & Wagnalls Standard Dictionary of Folklore, Mythology, and Legend* (Leach 1984, 710):

> Mermaids are usually depicted as having the head and body of a woman to the waist, and a tapering fish body and tail instead of legs. A carving on Puce Church in Gironde, France, however, shows a young mermaid with lower body divided and two tapering tails instead of legs. They live in an undersea world of splendor and riches, but have been known to assume human form and come ashore to markets and fairs. They often lure mariners to their destruction, and are said to gather the souls of the drowned and cage them in their domain. Those who seek fact underlying every belief have offered the manatee or the dugong, warm-blooded sea mammals, as the original for the mermaid, relying on analogy more than on sailors' ability to differentiate between a seacow and a fish-woman.

Of course, there was a male counterpart, the merman. (He was similar to Dagon, the god of the Philistines and later the Phoenicians, who was supposed—from uncertain mythological and etymological indications—to have been represented as half-man, half-fish. [*Benét's* 1987, 233].)

The folk traditions of the Canadian Maritimes—notably Nova Scotia, Prince Edward Island, and Newfoundland—include stories of both mermaids and mermen, as I have learned on several trips there. Once, in Nova Scotia, I purchased a folk-art mermaid of painted wood for my online Skeptiseum collection (see www.skeptiseum.org). And, for research before and during an investigative trip to Newfoundland (primarily for an appearance on the History Channel's *Monster Quest*, which aired in September 2008), I came across several mermaid tales (see, for example, Beck 1973, 249–50).

The oldest such account appeared in Captain Richard Whitbourne's *A Discourse and Discovery of New-found-land* published in 1620. The incident occurred in 1610. Whitbourne wrote:

> I espied veri[e] swiftly to come swimming towards me, looking cheerfully, as it had beene a woman, by the Face, Eyes, Nose, Mouth, Chin, Eares, Necke and Forehead: It seemed to be so beautifull, and in those parts so well proportioned, having round about upon the head, blew strakes, resembling haire, downe to the Necke. . . . I beheld the shoulders and backe downe to the middle, to be as square, white and smooth as the backe of a man, and from the middle to the hinder part, pointing in proportion like a b[roa]d hooked Arrow. . . . The same came shortly after unto a Boate, wherein one William Hawkridge, then my seruant, was . . . and the same Creature did put both his hands upon the side of the Boate, and did strive to come in to him and others then in the said Boate. . . . Whether it were a Maremaid or no, I know not; I leave it for others to judge. (quoted in Colombo 1988, 12–13)

Seal Maidens

It is difficult to say just what Whitbourne and others saw in the Newfoundland waters. No convincing mermaid or merman has ever washed up on shore. The usual explanation for mermaid sightings is the Dugong (*Dugongidae*), or Sea Cow, of the Indian Ocean. Along with manatees (*Trichechidae*) they are of the order *Sirenia*, which (notes an Audubon field guide to mammals) takes its name "from the supposed resemblance of its members to the mermaids, or sirens, of ancient myth" (Whitaker 1996,

805). However, it is unlikely that a sirenian would have been seen off the Newfoundland coast.

Whitbourne and his men may have seen a species of hair seal (family *Phocidae*) such as the Harbor Seal (*phoca vitulina*), which in my view would more closely match the Whitbourne mermaid than would a manatee. The harbor seal may indeed be white, have "blew strakes" (blue streaks) on its head, and the appearance of a mammal's face, shoulders, and "hands" (flippers) upon a fish's body (Whitaker 1996, 728–730 pl, 348). (It does not have external ears, but then eyewitness descriptions are often erroneous and can be affected by people's expectations.)

The possibility recalls the seal-maidens of Celtic folklore—creatures that could transform themselves from women to seals and back again (Levy 1999, 144). Among them, the *roane* was a type of fairy that wore seal skins to travel by sea; roanes could cast off the skins to go ashore and dance by moonlight. A less gentle type, the *skelkie*, would raise storms against seal hunters. Skelkies had large liquid eyes that made them lovelier than humans. According to legend, a male skelkie would occasionally mate with a human woman, producing a child with webbed fingers and toes (Conway 2002, 174, 178).

Fejee Mermaids

Famed showman P. T. Barnum acquired a "real" mermaid that had first been exhibited in 1822. Billing it as "the greatest curiosity in the world" he featured the "Fejee Mermaid" in his New York museum and then sent it on tour, exhibited alongside many genuine curiosities. Although he surely recognized that it was bogus from the beginning, and his museum naturalist proclaimed as much, Barnum was impressed at how closely it could be inspected without obvious signs of artifice.

Eventually there was a public outrage over the fake in South Carolina, and Barnum admitted that it was "a questionable, dead mermaid," telling his partner in the venture, Moses Kimball, "the bubble has burst" (Harris 1973, 22, 62–67; Kunhardt et al. 1995, 40–43).

Barnum's affair with the little mermaid taught him important lessons about human nature. Although the saying "There's a sucker born every minute" is *attributed* to him, there is no proof that he ever said it, and indeed, it seems a bit too harsh for Barnum's nature. Instead, he observed that many people enjoyed being fooled, and he often quoted the poem *Hudibras*: "Doubtless the pleasure is as great / Of being cheated as to cheat" (Kunhardt et al. 1995, 43; Keyes 1992, 6–7).

I have seen several "originals" of Barnum's Fejee Mermaid, although it presumably perished in the fire that consumed his museum in 1865. One of these is at Ripley's "Believe It or Not!" museum in Hollywood, its display card seeming to imply it is Barnum's own. Another is at Coney Island's sideshows, and still another is in Bobby Reynold's traveling sideshow museum. I once questioned Bobby about its authenticity as we stood together in his midway tent. He informed me, his eyes twinkling, that the curio had apparently been rescued by a fireman and passed down in his family. "And you believe that story?" I asked, good-naturedly. Bobby deadpanned that since he had paid several thousand dollars for it, he *had* to believe it (Nickell 2005, 336).

Taxidermed Fakes

It has also been claimed that Barnum's original Fejee mermaid was taken by Moses Kimball to Boston and from there made its way to the Peabody Museum (Kunhardt et al. 1995, 43). The one at the Peabody is actually known as the Java Mermaid. According to the *Harvard Gazette* (Early

Figure 21.1. "Fejee"-type mermaid (or merman?) was carefully examined by the author in a Vermont museum (photograph by the author).

1996), such fakes—which date back to the sixteenth century—were easily manufactured:

> For years experts believed that the "mermaids" were made by sewing together the head of a monkey and the tail of a fish. But in 1990, Peabody conservator Scott Fulton conducted a full-scale examination. Fulton ran starch tests on the Java Mermaid's front section. "We discovered that it is made of papier-mâché molded to resemble the limbs of the creature," he says. Then he showed the creature to Karel Liem, professor of ichthyology, and Karsten Hartel, curatorial associate in ichthyology at the Museum of Comparative Zoology. "It was the ingenuity of the thing, the way it was put together that I remember," says Hartel, who confirmed that the creature's composure [*sic*] included real fish parts. According to Fulton's records, the mermaid's teeth, fingernails, and fins, are nothing more than the jaws and the teeth, spines, and fins of a carp and a porgy-like fish, "placed liberally."

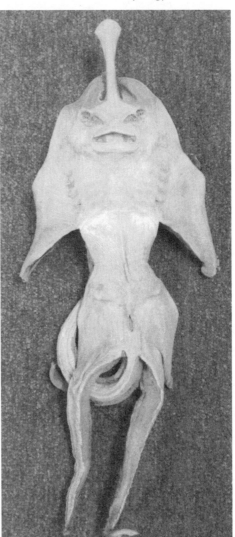

This analysis is similar to my own, conducted on a specimen at the Nature Museum in Grafton, Vermont, on August 31, 2003. It was generously made available to me by curator Steven Lorenz. I first photographed it (see figure 21.1), then examined it using a 10X illuminated loupe (a small mag-

Figure 21.2. A "Jenny Hanniver" is a manufactured mermaid—in this case made by altering a devilfish (author's collection).

nifier such as that used by jewelers). The real-fish hind part was joined to an upper body molded of some composition material (I did not remove samples for analysis); the hair was glued on, the teeth inserted, and the claws affixed.

To the eye at least, the Grafton mermaid is almost indistinguishable from a "Merman of Aden" exhibited at the former Ripley's "Believe It Or Not!" odditorium in New York City. In my collection is a 1939 postcard picturing the creature—even in the same pose as the Grafton one—noting that "In Aden on the Red Sea, Mr. Ripley found a 'merman' which he judges to be a clever oriental fake . . ." ("Merman" 1939).

Another type of manufactured mermaid, known as a "Jenny Haniver," was created by making alterations to a devilfish (Stein 1993, 260–61). I have seen more than one of these exhibited in a carnival sideshow (Nickell 2005, 336), while another is in my personal collection (see figure 21.2).

References

Beck, Horace. 1973. *Folklore and the Sea*. Edison, NJ: Castle Books.

Colombo, John Robert. 1988. *Mysterious Canada: Strange Sights, Extraordinary Events, and Peculiar Places*. Toronto: Doubleday Canada.

Conway, D. J. 2002. *Magical, Mystical Creatures*. 2nd ed. St. Paul, MN: Llewellyn Publications.

Early, Andrea. 1996. "The Little Mermaid?" *Harvard University Gazette*, October 17.

Harris, Neil. 1973. *Humbug: The Art of P. T. Barnum*. Chicago, IL: University of Chicago Press.

Kunhardt, Philip B., Jr., et al. 1995. *P. T. Barnum: America's Greatest Showman*. New York: Alfred A. Knopf.

Keyes, Ralph. 1992. *"Nice Guys Finish Seventh": False Phrases, Spurious Sayings, and Familiar Quotations*. New York: HarperPerennial.

Leach, Maria, ed. 1984. *Funk & Wagnalls Standard Dictionary of Folklore, Mythology, and Legend*. New York: Harper & Row.

Levy, Joel, ed. 1999. *A Natural History of the Unnatural World*. New York: St. Martin's Press.

Merman of Aden. 1939. Ripley odditorium postcard. New York: National Postcard Headquarters.

Nickell, Joe. 2005. *Secrets of the Sideshows*. Lexington, KY: University Press of Kentucky.

Stein, Gordon. 1993. *Encyclopedia of Hoaxes*. Detroit, MI: Gale Research.

Whitaker, John O., Jr. 1996. *National Audubon Society Field Guide to North American Mammals*. New York: Alfred A. Knopf.

Chapter 22

Lure of Swamp Creatures

According to much evidence that has been shown over the years, strange, quasi-humanlike beings are supposed to inhabit swamplands of the southern United States. Eyewitness encounters and web-toed footprints suggest a type of hybrid creature—possibly "a cross between a Primate and a large alligator" (Davis 2008, 2). Unfortunately, science holds that such a hybridization would be impossible, but then how do we explain the appearances and tracks of creatures that thus far have eluded mainstream science?

Honey Island Swamp Monster

Louisiana's Honey Island Swamp Monster debuted in 1974 when a pair of local hunters emerged from a remote backwater area with plaster casts of "unusual tracks." The duo claimed they discovered the tracks close to a wild boar that lay dead with a gashed throat. The hunters also stated that in 1963 they had seen similar tracks after they had encountered an awesome creature. It stood seven feet tall, was covered with grayish hair, and had large, amber-colored eyes, the men said. However, the creature promptly ran away and an afternoon rainstorm obliterated its tracks, they claimed.

The men were Harlan E. Ford and Billy Mills, who worked together as air-traffic controllers. Ford appeared on an episode of the television series *In Search of . . .* during the 1970s. His granddaughter, Dana Holy-field (1999a, 11), recalled:

> When the documentary was first televised, it was monster mania around here. People called from everywhere. . . . The legend of the Honey Island Swamp Monster escalated across Southern Louisiana and quickly made its way out of state after the documentary aired nationwide.

Until his death in 1980, Harlan Ford continued to search for the monster. Dana recalls how he once took a goat into the swamp to use as bait, hoping to lure the creature to a tree blind. There Ford waited, uneventfully, with his gun and camera. He claimed to find several different-sized tracks on one hunting trip and to see the creature on one other occasion (during a fishing trip with Mills and some of their friends). Reportedly one of the men then went searching for the creature and managed to fire two shots at it before returning to the campfire (Holyfield 1999a, 10–15).

Investigating on Site

I was intrigued by the monster reports, and I was able to pursue them on a trip to New Orleans in 2000 (after I spoke to local skeptics at the planetarium in Kenner). Indeed, I was determined to visit the alleged creature's habitat; the Honey Island Swamp (see figure 22.1) which comprises nearly 70,000 acres between the East and West Pearl rivers. I signed on with a tour operated out of Slidell, Louisiana, by wetlands ecologist Paul Wagner and his wife, Sue. Their Honey Island Swamp Tours live up to their billing as explorations of "the deeper, harder-to-reach small bayous and sloughs" of "one of the wildest and most pristine river swamps in America" ("Dr. Wagner's" n.d.).

Asked about the monster's existence, the Wagners are ambivalent. Although they have seen alligators, bobcats, otters, and numerous other species, they have not found a trace of the alleged creature (Wagner 2000). Neither has Captain Robbie Charbonnet, the Wagners' Cajun guide. Beginning at age eight, Charbonnet acquired forty-five years' experience in the Honey Island Swamp, eighteen as a guide. Responding to my query, he insisted that he had "never seen or heard" anything that could be attributed to a monster (Charbonnet 2000).

Throughout our tour, in fact, Charbonnet repeatedly identified species after species in the isolated swamp, skillfully navigating his boat through the tupelos and cypresses hung with Spanish moss. Even though the cool

Figure 22.1. Louisiana's pristine Honey Island Swamp is the alleged habitat of a humanlike monster (photograph by the author).

weather had sent alligators to the depths, the guide pointed out great blue herons, turtles, and other wildlife. From merely glimpsing a silhouette, he identified a barred owl, then carefully steered for a closer view. He pointed to traces of other creatures, calling attention to branches freshly cut by beavers and, in the mud, wild boar tracks. But there was neither hide nor hair nor track of the Honey Island Swamp Monster.

Naturalist John V. Dennis is another skeptic of monster claims. As he wrote in *The Great Cypress Swamps* (1988): "Honey Island has achieved fame of sorts because of the real or imagined presence of a creature that fits the description of the Big Foot of movie renown. Known as the Thing, the creature is sometimes seen by fishermen." However, Dennis says, "For my part, let me say that in my many years of visiting swamps, many of them as wild or wilder than Honey Island, I have never obtained a glimpse of anything vaguely resembling Big Foot, nor have I ever seen suspicious-looking footprints." The naturalist concludes, "Honey Island, in my experience, does not live up to its reputation as a scary place."

Nevertheless, contrasting with the absence of monster experiences from swamp experts are the claims of Harlan Ford and Billy Mills. Those purported eyewitnesses are, in investigators' parlance, "repeaters"—

people who claim unusual experiences on multiple occasions. (For instance, recall Roger Patterson [chapter 6]. Before he shot his film sequence of a hairy man-beast in 1967, he was a longtime Sasquatch buff who had repeatedly "discovered" the alleged creature's tracks [Bord and Bord 1982, 80].) Ford's and Mills's multiple encounters seem suspiciously lucky, and suspicions are increased by other evidence, including the tracks.

I obtained from Dana Holyfield an exact plaster copy of one of the several track casts her grandfather made (see figure 22.2). Clearly, it is not the track of a typical Bigfoot whose prints are "roughly human in design," as noted by anthropologist and pro-Sasquatch theorist Grover Krantz (1992, 17). Ford's monster instead leaves web-toed tracks, seemingly "a cross between a primate and a large alligator" (Holyfield 1999a, 9). The footprint is also surprisingly small: only about nine and three-fourths inches long compared to those of Bigfoot, which average about fourteen to sixteen inches (Coleman and Clark 1999, 14), with some tracks of over twenty inches having been reported (Coleman and Huyghe 1999).*

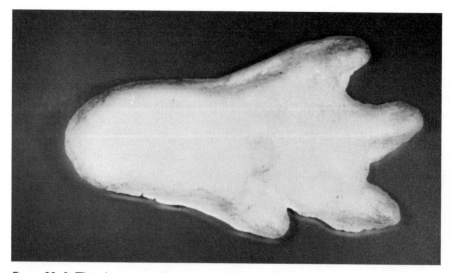

Figure 22. 2. This plaster cast preserves an alleged Honey Island Swamp Monster track (author's collection).

---

*While Harlan Ford exhibited different-sized tracks, a photograph of his mounted casts (Holyfield 1999a, 10) allows them to be compared with his open hand which, touching the display, thus gives an approximate scale. This shows all are relatively small. The cast I obtained from Dana Holyfield, Ford's granddaughter, is consistent with the larger ones.

Domain of the Monsters

Ford and Mills's monster is clearly not a Bigfoot, a fact that robs their story of any credibility it might have had from that association. Monster buffs instead link the Honey Island reports to other "North American 'Creatures of the Black Lagoon' cases," which allege evidence of entities dubbed "freshwater Merbeings" (Coleman and Huyghe 1999, 39, 62). These creatures are linked, supposedly by tracks with three toes, although Harlan Ford's casts actually exhibit four (again see figure 22.2). In short, the purported Honey Island Swamp Monster is unique, rare even among creatures whose existence is unproven and unlikely.

Putting aside footprints and other specific details, the Honey Island Swamp Monster can be viewed as one of a type of mythic swamp-dwelling "beastmen" or "manimals." These include South Carolina's Scape Ore Swamp Lizardman; the smelly Skunk Ape and hybrid Gatorman of Florida's Everglades and other southern swamplands; Momo, the Missouri Monster; and others, including the Fouke Monster, which peered in the window of a home in Fouke, Arkansas, one night in 1971, setting off a monster-sighting scare (Blackman 1998, 23–25, 30–33, 166–68; Bord and Bord 1982, 104–105; Coleman and Clark 1999, 224–26; Coleman and Huyghe 1999, 39, 56).

But why swamps and why monsters? Swamplands represent isolated, unexplored regions, which have traditionally been the domain of legendary creatures. As noted biologist John Napier (1973, 23) of the Smithsonian Institution sagely observed, monsters "hail from uncharted territory: inaccessible mountains, impenetrable forests, remote Pacific islands, the depths of loch or ocean. . . . The essential element of the monster myth is remoteness."

Likewise, in commenting on one reported Honey Island Swamp encounter, John V. Dennis (1988) observes: "In many cases, sightings such as this one are inspired by traditions that go back as far as Indian days. If a region is wild and inaccessible and has a history of encounters with strange forms of life, chances are that similar encounters will occur again—or at least be reported." And considering that Bigfoot's supposed major domain is the Pacific northwest, the late anthropologist Grover Krantz (1992, 199) observed: "Many of the more persistent eastern reports come from low-lying and/or swampy lands of the lower Mississippi and other major river basins."

Robbie Charbonnet, my Cajun guide, shared some insights about such entities as the Honey Island Swamp Monster. He said that frightening tales could sometimes have been concocted to keep outsiders away—to safeguard prime hunting territory or even possibly to help protect moonshine stills. Charbonnet also suggested that such stories served in a bogeyman fashion, frightening children so they would keep away from dangerous areas. (When he was a boy, he recalled, an uncle would describe a scary figure, with one leg, a mutilated face, etc., that would be sure to "get" him if he strayed into the wilderness.)

As with other bogeymen, the Honey Island Swamp Monster is ideal for prompting campfire chills. One narrative relates, "A group of men were sitting around the campfire along the edge of the Pearl River, telling stories about that thing in the swamp . . ." (Holyfield 1999b). There is a song, "The Honey Island Swamp Monster" (Perry Ford n.d.), which begins: "Late at night by a dim fire light, / You people best beware. / He's standing in the shadows, / Lurking around out there. . . ." The alleged creature has even been referred to specifically as "The boogie man" and even "that booger" (Holyfield 1992a, 14)—"booger" being a dialect form of *bogey*, and stories intended to scare being sometimes called "'booger' tales" (Cassidy 1985).

Among the available subjects for booger tales are the many Louisiana bayou and swamp terrors that are products of Cajun folklore. For instance, there is the Letiche, a ghoul that supposedly began as an abandoned, illegitimate child who was reared by alligators and has morphed into a creature with webbed hands and feet, scaly skin, and glowing, green eyes. Another is Jack O'Lantern, an evil spirit who lures people into deadly swamps by mesmerizing them with his lantern. In addition, there is the legendary loup-garou (a Cajun werewolf—see chapter 10), as well as zombies (not the essentially harmless "Voodoo Zombies" but the terrifying "Flesh Eaters") (Blackman 1998, 171–209).

Swamp creatures also serve as subjects for horror fiction. For example, the Fouke monster sightings inspired the 1972 horror film, *The Legend of Boggy Creek*, which became a box-office hit and spawned a sequel and many imitations. About this time also emerged a popular series of comic books titled *Swamp Thing* that featured a metamorphosing man-beast from a Louisiana swamp. Revealingly, these popularized monsters predated the 1974 claims of Ford and Mills (their alleged earlier encounter of 1963 not yet having been reported).

Making Tracks

Although such horrific man-beasts remain unproven, hoaxers certainly do exist (Dennett 1982). No fewer than seven Bigfoot hoaxes were launched during the early 1970s by a man named Ray Pickens of Chehalis, Washington. Pickens carved primitive seven-by-eighteen-inch feet and attached them to hiking boots. He said he was motivated "not to fool the scientists, but to fool the monster-hunters" who he felt regarded people like him as "hicks" (Pickens 1975). Further incentive, according to monster enthusiast Peter Byrne (1975), derives from the "extraordinary psychology of people wanting to get their names in the paper, people wanting a little publicity, wanting to be noticed."

Was this the motivation for Harlan Ford's and Billy Mills's monster claims? Dana Holyfield (1999a, 5–6) says in her grandfather's defense: "Harlan wasn't a man to make up something like that. He was down-to-earth and honest and told it the way it was and didn't care if people believed him or not." Yet even a fundamentally honest person, who would never do anything overtly reprehensible, might engage in behavior he considered harmless and essentially fun. Indeed, the evidence indicates that Ford and Mills did just that. In summary, there are the pair's suspicious repeated sightings and track discoveries coupled with the incongruent mixing of a Bigfoot-type beast with very un-Bigfoot-like feet. As well, the evidence they provided was just the type that could easily be faked and, indeed, often has been. Moreover, their claims occur in the context of a mythology of swamp manimals that has many antecedent elements in both folklore and fiction. All in all, the evidence suggests common hoaxing.

In fact, since my investigation, one of a pair of "shoes" for making swamp-monster tracks was discovered partially buried in mud near Harlan Ford's former hunting camp. The form and size of the attached resin-cast "foot" are comparable to Ford's notorious tracks. It is offset from the shoe, apparently by a wood block, so the foot would flex and thus give a realistic impression, while the shoe itself remained clear of the tracks ("Harlan" 2008; "Legend" 2008).

Other Hoaxes

There is no doubt that, in the wake of the monster hype Harlan Ford helped to inspire, considerable hoaxing took place. According to Holyfield (1999a, 11), "Then there were the monster impersonators who made fake

Bigfoot shoes and tromped through the swamp. This went on for years. Harlan didn't worry about the jokers because he knew the difference." In any event, swamp-monster hoaxes—known and apparent—continue.

Only a few months before my trip to Louisiana, two loggers, Carl Dubois and Earl Whitstine, reported encountering a man-beast in a cypress swamp known as Boggy Bayou in the central part of the state. Giant four-toed tracks and hair samples were discovered at the site, and soon others came forward to say they too had seen a similar creature. However, there were grounds for suspicion: twenty-five years earlier (i.e., not long after the 1974 Honey Island Swamp Monster reports), Whitstine's father and some friends had sawed giant foot shapes from plywood and produced fake monster tracks in the woods of a nearby parish (Blanchard 2000; Burdeau 2000).

Laboratory tests of the hair from the Boggy Bayou creature—a bogeyman I have dubbed Boggyman—were conducted on September 13, 2000, revealing that it was not *Gigantopithecus blacki* (a scientific name for Sasquatch proposed by Krantz [1992, 193], but more like *Booger louisiani* (my term for the legendary swamp bogeyman). It actually proved to be from *Equus caballus* (a horse), whereupon the local sheriff's department promptly ended its investigation (Blanchard 2000; Burdeau 2000).

Harlan Ford reportedly believed that the swamp monsters "were probably on the verge of extinction" (Holyfield 1999a, 10). He certainly did much to promote belief in them. I suspect that—so long as suitably remote habitats exist, along with other essentials (including campfires around which to gather and spin tales and good ol' boys seeking their fifteen minutes of fame)—the legendary swamp monsters will continue to thrive.

References

Baker, Robert A. 1995. Afterword to Nickell, 1995, pp. 275–85 (below).

Blackman, W. Haden. 1998. *The Field Guide to North American Monsters.* New York: Three Rivers Press.

Blanchard, Kevin. 2000. "Bigfoot Sighting in La.?" *Advocate* (Baton Rouge, LA), August 29.

Bord, Janet, and Colin Bord. 1982. *The Bigfoot Casebook.* Harrisburg, PA: Stackpole Books.

Burdeau, Cain. 2000. "Many in Central La. Fear Bigfoot." *Advocate* (Baton Rouge, LA), September 15.

Byrne, Peter. 1975. Quoted in Guenette and Guenette 1975, p. 81 (below).

Cassidy, Frederick G., ed. 1985. *Dictionary of American Regional English.* Cambridge, MA: Belknap Press, pp. 1:333–34.

Charbonnet, Robbie. 2000. Interview by the author. December 4.

Coleman, Loren, and Jerome Clark. 1999. *Cryptozoology A to Z*. New York: Fireside (Simon & Schuster).

Coleman, Loren, and Patrick Huyghe. 1999. *The Field Guide to Bigfoot, Yeti, and Other Mystery Primates Worldwide*. New York: Avon, pp. 14–19.

Dennett, Michael. 1982. "Bigfoot Jokester Reveals Punchline—Finally." *Skeptical Inquirer* 7, no. 1 (Fall): 8–9.

Dennis, John V. 1988. *The Great Cypress Swamps*. Baton Rouge, LA: Louisiana State University Press, pp. 27, 108–109.

"Dr. Wagner's Honey Island Swamp Tours, Inc." N.d. Advertising flyer, Slidell, LA.

Ford, Perry. N.d. "The Honey Island Swamp Monster." Song text in Holyfield 1999b, p. 13 (below).

Guenette, Robert, and Frances Guenette. 1975. *The Mysterious Monsters*. Los Angeles, CA: Sun Classic Pictures.

Davis, M. K., and Jay Michael. "Harlan Ford's Cast Is Fake?" http://jmichaelms.tripod.com/HIS/suspect.htm (accessed December 31, 2008).

Holyfield, Dana. 1999a. *Encounters with the Honey Island Swamp Monster*. Pearl River, LA: Honey Island Swamp Books.

———. 1999b. *More Swamp Cookin' with the River People*. Pearl River, LA: Honey Island Swamp Books.

Krantz. Grover. 1992. *Big Footprints: A Scientific Inquiry into the Reality of Sasquatch*. Boulder, CO: Johnson Books.

"Legend of the Honey Island Swamp Monster." http://www.bigfootforums.com/ (accessed December 31, 2008).

Nickell, Joe. 1995. *Entities: Angels, Spirits, Demons, and Other Alien Beings*. Amherst, NY: Prometheus Books.

Pickens, Ray. 1975. Quoted in Guenette and Guenette 1975, p. 80 (above).

Wagner, Sue. 2000. Interview by the author. December 4.

Afterword

Many of the man-beasts we have looked at seem headed for extinction. Two types—Bigfoot and the humanoid alien—still thrive as powerfully mythic beings.

As our planet "shrinks," with wilderness places becoming fewer and less remote, hairy man-beasts survive mythologically, perceived as evolutionary throwbacks, endangered species of an imperiled planet. Bigfoot is an "ecomessiah," states anthropologist David J. Daegling (2004, 250). "If it survives, nature survives."

And as we turn from Bigfoot, a metaphor of our past, we look ahead to the frontiers of the universe with its mythological, futuristic-appearing humanoids. Various "contactees" and "abductees" claim to have received messages (often telepathically) from extraterrestrials—messages like one about "the danger facing the earth's ecology" (Mack 1994, 381).

At a time when old myths are in decline, we stand witness to vibrant new ones, spawned by concerns for our planet and our place in the cosmos. These are developing before our very eyes. While sometimes the mythic beings are bogeymen, representing our primal fears, at other times they are expressive of hope, prophetic beings offering us a type of salvation. One can only wish the latter really did exist.

References

Daegling, David J. 2004. *Bigfoot Exposed*. New York: Rowman & Littlefield Publications.

Mack, John. 1994. *Abduction: Human Encounters with Aliens*. New York: Simon & Schuster.

Appendix

The North American Bigfoot

Image and Myth

published compilation of American and Canadian Sasquatch sightings—from 1818 to November 1980—reveals an astonishing variation of physical descriptions, footprint shapes, and geographical distribution (Bord and Bord 2006, 215–310). However, these are tending toward standardization as the supposed creature—dubbed Bigfoot in 1958—develops into a significant modern mythology.

Habitat

The distribution, for example, begins with the earliest ("possibly fictional") report in Maine, and includes most of continental America's states (excepting Delaware, Rhode Island, and South Carolina) and eight of thirteen Canadian provinces. The greatest number of sightings were in Washington state (110), followed by California (104), British Columbia (90), and Oregon (77)—that is, in the Pacific Northwest—followed by Pennsylvania and Florida (42 each), Ohio (40), and Illinois and Iowa (27 each). The creatures were reportedly seen in woodlands, on beaches, in swamps and fields, along roadsides, in the Mohave Desert, on a rocky crag, in a citrus grove, and elsewhere. In at least one instance in 1974, the creature was "inside a UFO."

In many instances an alleged creature was known by a particular name in the area in which it was reported. Consider, for example, the following:

- "Big Muddy Monster"—Reported in 1973–1974 at the Big Muddy River near Murphysboro, Illinois. Not surprisingly, the seven-foot, white Bigfoot had "muddy body hair."
- "Brush Ape"—Appearing in Pacific, Missouri, in 1975 but similar to creatures reported in Missouri since 1925, and possibly equated with the notorious "Momo" (Missouri Monster) of 1972. (See Coleman and Huyghe 1999, 50–51.)
- The "Dwayo" (or Dwayyo)—described as a "huge hairy creature." It has been seen "from time to time" in the 1920s in Maryland, in the area of Gambrill State Park.
- "Fouke Monster"—sighted around Fouke, Arkansas, beginning in 1953, and 1973, a four- to eight-foot Bigfoot with black hair. It was the inspiration for the *Legend of Boggy Creek* movies (Coleman and Huyghe 1999, 56–57).
- "Skunk Ape"—the term for Florida's Bigfoot, which has a gorilla-like appearance and an especially strong smell. It has been reported especially since the 1970s (when developers encroached on the Everglades). Descriptions vary, or as cryptozoologist Loren Coleman (1999, 224) says, "there seems to be more than one kind of Skunk Ape."
- "White Demon"—A white to grayish-white Bigfoot seen in central Washington in 1961 and again in 1966–1970. (Its prototype may have been a "Bigfoot with longish, dirty-white hair" reported at Mount St. Helens in 1955 or 1956.)
- "Yellow Top"—Also known as "Old Yellow Top," a dark, bearlike animal with a light-colored mane. It has been reported near Cobalt, Ontario, since 1906 (with notable sightings in 1923, 1946, and 1970) (see also Coleman and Huyghe 1999, 48–49).

Developing Iconography

As even these few examples begin to suggest, if a single type of creature is represented by the myriad sightings, it is truly chameleonesque. Eyewitnesses describe it as ranging in color from white to gray, silver-gray, silver and charcoal, gray-blue, yellow, "the color of a collie dog," brown, dark brown with silver-tipped hair, reddish, and often black. Its hair "stood upright" or was long and straight, curly, or "slimy." In two cases the creature had fishlike scales. At times its eyes were green, red—even "glowing"—and "amber reflecting." Its height ranged from as little as eighteen inches to occasionally four and often six to seven feet, or as tall as eight, nine, or even ten feet. One witness reported it as fifteen feet tall.

Its form also varied. It was characterized often as a "wild man" (for example, with "long matted hair and a beard"), but was also described as a "baboon" or "giant gorilla," a "devil," "half-man, half-beast," a hairy "booger," a "bearlike" creature, "half bear, half gorillia," a "cross between dog and ape" (with "human head and shoulders"), and so on. A 1972 Ohio sighting featured a six- to eight-foot creature "with wolflike head, elongated nose, red eyes, fangs, and huge feet." In another case that year, in Oregon, the beast had a "pointed head and no neck." In Lancaster, Pennsylvania, in 1973, two brothers saw a gray Bigfoot that had a white mane as well as curved horns, together with "tigerlike fangs" and "long grizzly claws" (Bord and Bord 2006, 215–310).

Its tracks were equally varied. There were three-toed, fifteen-inch footprints; an eleven-inch handprint and sixteen-inch footprints with four toes; five-toed tracks, twenty inches long by seven inches wide; and many other variations, including six-toed tracks (for more on Bigfoot prints, see Daegling 2004, 157–87).

As to behavior, it yelled, screamed, screeched, howled, growled, wailed, gurgled, "chattered its teeth," and so on. It walked upright or on all fours. It smelled musty or even putrid. It pursued cattle, hunted rabbits with a club, made fire, picked berries, peered frequently into windows, treated an Indian for snakebite, wrestled with other Bigfoot, walked holding its youngster by the hand, sat on a log, and—among other actions—fled from people or (on several occasions) kidnapped them. For instance, a camper named Albert Ostman claimed that in 1924 he was kept prisoner by a family of Bigfoot until he was able to escape—an incident he did not report until 1957—"at a time" (according to Bord and Bord 2006, 42) "when Bigfoot was in the news."

Bigfoot was often fired at but (hoaxes aside) never, apparently, more than wounded—except once, when its body was allegedly examined and then left behind! In one instance, after being shot at, the creature "changed shape and vanished." Small wonder that Bigfooters have suggested, "Bigfoot can't be killed" (Bord and Bord 2006, 51–70).

Evolution into Myth

Bigfoot seems slowly to have evolved—imaginatively—into a mythical being. (Essentially, a myth is a story presenting supernormal episodes that are powerfully explanatory [*Benét's* 1987, 678]).

In the early reports, "wild man" sightings were common, along with "gorillalike" animals and a spectrum of man-beasts of varied descriptions. Hoaxes became increasingly common.

Reports increased in the 1950s. The photograph of an alleged Yeti footprint in late 1951 in the Himalayan mountains and the subsequent media focus on the "abominable snowman" helped boost the Sasquatch legend as well as the number of the alleged creature's tracks. It was rechristened Bigfoot in 1958 (Daegling 2004, 29, 73).

After illustrations of Bigfoot began increasingly to appear in books, and especially after Roger Patterson's 1967 color film was widely circulated, the image of what Bigfoot "really" looked like began to tend toward standardization. As I discovered in travels with investigator Vaughn Rees throughout "Bigfoot Country" in northern California, artists—who render the creature's image in murals, giant chainsaw carvings, and other effigies, especially on souvenirs—know instinctively to proceed like artists who portray other mythic likenesses (of Jesus, Santa Claus, etc.): Stay within accepted parameters if you wish the image to be easily recognized and appreciated. I therefore suspect that the white Bigfoot and the Bigfoot with horns, for example, are especially endangered species.

And *speaking* of endangered species, author Ken Wylie (1980, 224–35) recognized belief in Bigfoot as representing a modern myth relating to ecology. Anthropologist David J. Daegling (2004, 248) observes that believers "see Bigfoot as, among other things, an ecological messiah" or "ecomessiah." As he elaborates (2004, 25):

> We seem incapable of fulfilling our own needs without destroying some aspect of nature; we have neither the collective will nor the wisdom to preserve the wilderness. Kenneth Wylie suggests that the Sasquatch serves to remind us that the subjugation of nature comes at a cost. It is no accident that Bigfoot is perceived as existing between the realms of human and animal: How many Bigfoot encounters have ended when the hunter declared that he could not shoot the creature because it was simply too human? Bigfoot, its limitless potential maintained by its mystery, is the ideal guardian of nature. If we destroy Bigfoot, we kill part of ourselves— that core of our being that was once part of nature but then evolved out of it. Certainly one part of the appeal and persistence of Bigfoot is that it is put into the role of the ecological savior. If it survives, nature survives. We can catch a fleeting glimpse of our connection to the earth, our origins in the raw wilderness, if Bigfoot remains in our midst.

As our planet "shrinks," with wilderness places becoming fewer and less remote, hairy man-beasts seem to survive as a mythical remnant of our endangered planet. We look back to "Bigfoot" with many of the same impulses that cause us to look ahead to the unexplored universe and its imagined futuristic-appearing humanoids. At a time when the old mythologies (including the great religions) are in decline, we find ourselves at a new, mythmaking crossroads.

References

Benét's Reader's Encyclopedia. 1987. New York: Harper & Row.

Bord, Janet, and Colin Bord. 2006. *Bigfoot Casebook Updated*. N.p.: Pine Winds Press.

Coleman, Loren. 1999. *Crytozoology A to Z*. New York: Fireside.

Coleman, Loren, and Patrick Huyghe. 1999. *The Field Guide to Bigfoot, Yeti, and Other Mystery Primates Worldwide*. New York: Avon Books.

Daegling, David J. 2004. *Bigfoot Exposed: An Anthropologist Examines America's Enduring Legend*. New York: AltaMira Press.

Hendricks, Rhoda A. 1963. *Mythology Pocket Crammer*. New York: Ken Publishing.

Wylie, Kenneth. 1980. *Bigfoot: A Personal Inquiry into a Phenomenon*. New York: Viking Press.

Index

Note: Italicized page numbers indicate illustrations.